THE
ALMOST
VEGETARIAN
COOKBOOK

SAINSBURY'S

THE
ALMOST
VEGETARIAN
COOKBOOK

JOSCELINE DIMBLEBY

Photography by Simon Wheeler

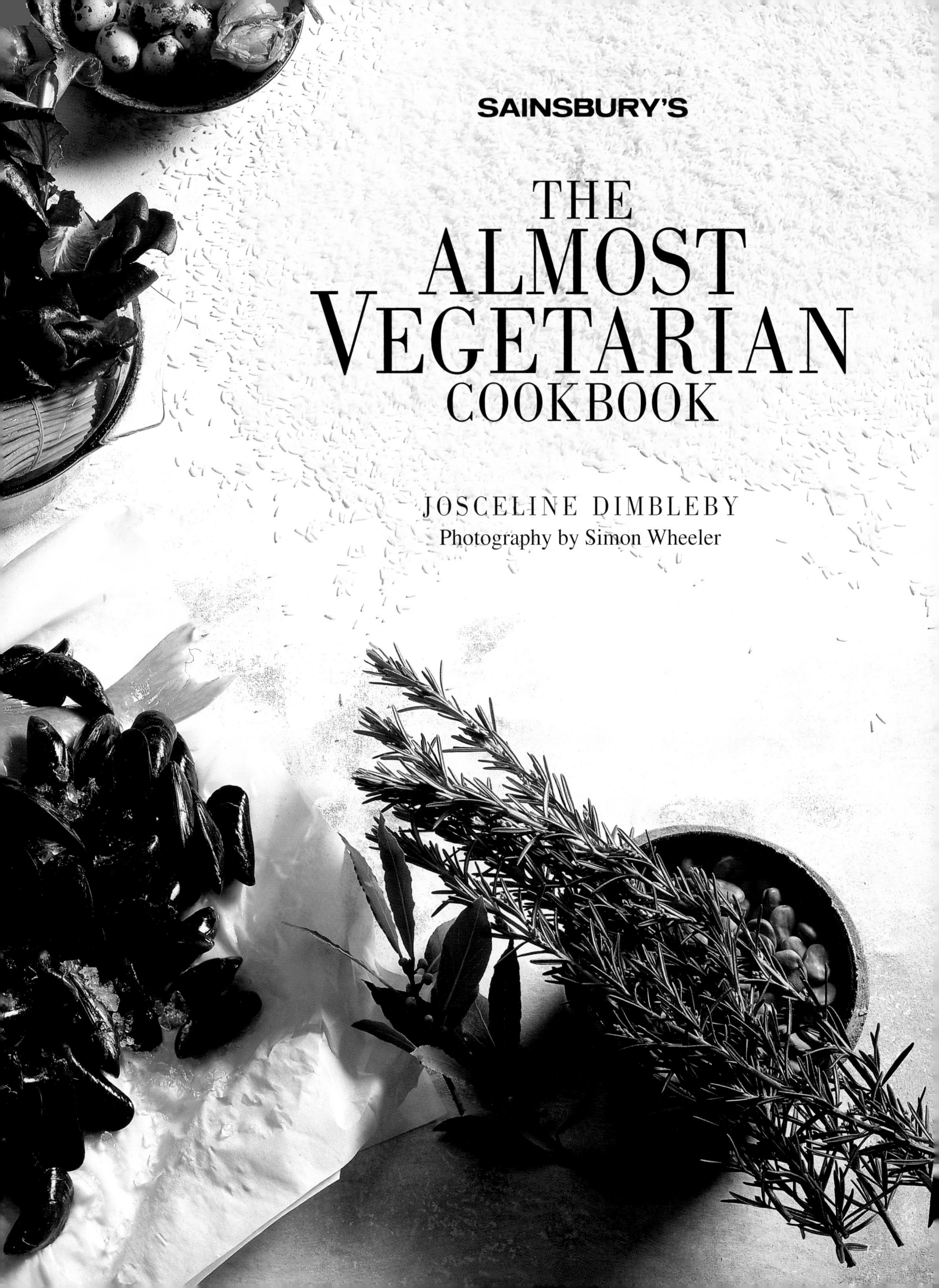

Published in the UK exclusively for J Sainsbury plc,
Stamford House, Stamford Street, London SE1 9LL
by Websters International Publishers Limited,
Axe & Bottle Court, 70 Newcomen Street, London SE1 1YT

First published 1994
Copyright © 1994 Websters International Publishers
Text copyright © 1994 Josceline Dimbleby
Photographs copyright © 1994 Websters International Publishers

ISBN 1 870604 13 X

Colour separation by Columbia Offset, Singapore
Printed and bound by Dai Nippon Printing, Hong Kong

Conceived, edited and designed by Websters International Publishers

NOTES ON RECIPES
All spoon measures are level unless otherwise stated
1 tablespoon = 15ml
1 teaspoon = 5ml

Eggs are size 3 unless otherwise stated.
Pepper is freshly ground black pepper unless otherwise stated.
Milk is full-fat fresh milk unless otherwise stated.
When using agar-agar flakes as a substitute for gelatine, follow the instructions on the packet -
the equivalent quantities given in the recipes are approximate

Raw Eggs some recipes in this book contain raw eggs. Because of the danger of infection in eggs from
salmonella bacteria, however, we recommend that raw or lightly cooked eggs are not served to
pregnant women, babies, small children or elderly people.

Ovens should be preheated to the specified temperature.
For all recipes, quantities are given in both metric and imperial measures.
Follow either metric or imperial measures but not a mixture of both.

► Opposite page, left to right:
*Peppers filled with garlic potatoes and cooked in olive oil (107); Vietnamese chicken
noodle hot pot with fresh leaves (95); carrot tart with candied carrot topping (139)*

CONTENTS

INTRODUCTION

I don't think I shall ever become a total vegetarian. My love of all food, of the wonderful variety now available, and of my freedom to try anything, would stop me. However, I have noticed that these days I eat far less meat and, indeed, don't miss it at all even when I haven't touched it for weeks. Vegetarianism has increased enormously over recent years but so, perhaps even more, has the number of people who have reduced their consumption of red meat to almost nothing, and concentrate instead on eating far more vegetables, as well as poultry and fish dishes which are combined with a large proportion of vegetables, or with grains such as rice or bulgar, with pasta or with pulses. In this way, they easily consume less animal fat and feel healthier and more energetic: in fact, the 'almost vegetarian' diet could be considered to provide the best of both worlds.

My philosophy of eating is a very straightforward – even old-fashioned – one. I am a firm believer that any normally healthy person is wisest to eat the most varied diet they can, remembering only the simple rule that they can eat what they want, but never too much of any one thing. There are so many different diets suggested nowadays that people with no specific medical reason to restrict themselves are sometimes persuaded to try a complicated way of eating – to cut out this or that ingredient or type of food often on the slightest of pretexts. This sort of thing induces worry, and worry is not healthy. We have to eat to live and luckily good food is one of the great joys of life; it promotes a feeling of happiness and well-being – and happiness is most definitely healthy.

I do love vegetables, with their magnificent variety of appetizing colours, textures and flavours, and this book has therefore been a great pleasure to work on. I have one vegetarian daughter and several vegetarian friends, and this gave me particular inspiration when dreaming up the strictly vegetable main dishes. The increasing availability of different kinds of vegetables offers endless scope for interesting combinations, and

◀ *Cod with sorrel and spinach purée in puff pastry packets (p83)*

vegetables can truly be a feast for the eye as well as the stomach. Gone are the days when all vegetarian dishes seemed to be varying shades of brown.

Salads in particular have become much more interesting. We now have at our disposal not only some truly wonderful salad leaves but also nut oils and fruit and herb vinegars to combine with spices and seasonings in exciting dressings.

A large variety of pulses, grains and rice as well as both eggs and cheese greatly extend the culinary possibilities for any vegetarian. They also help to replace the proteins that would otherwise be provided by meat-based dishes. They are also extremely useful for informal meals of any kind. Pasta has of course become an absolutely vital part of almost everyone's life; what would we do, arriving home late and tired to an almost empty fridge, if we did not have that packet of tagliatelle on the shelf and a bottle of extra virgin olive oil?

When it is really fresh and carefully cooked, fish is probably always my first choice. I still think of it as the 'brain food' I was told it was as a child, and it never makes you feel weighed down or bloated. The flavours are delicate, and textures light and succulent, and these days again there is a wider range of fish and shellfish available than ever before.

All kinds of poultry are a boon to the family cook. Inexpensive, versatile and loved by children, it is a great stand-by. Poultry adapts to almost any added ingredients or flavourings, and as you will see from my recipes, poultry dishes can be transformed into mild, homely dishes or something excitingly exotic, to suit your mood.

I could not produce any comprehensive collection of recipes without a large selection of puddings. Puddings are my passion: fruit puddings, chocolate puddings, ice creams, gooey cakes – in fact, all kinds of puddings. I know that puddings cannot be said to be strictly necessary to a healthy diet, but they are fun to make and a supreme pleasure to eat. The occasional indulgence is not going to do you any harm and will almost certainly do a great deal to lift your spirits.

STARTERS & SOUPS

The start of a meal is crucial. It sets the tone, and is often the most remembered dish. Appetites are keen and your guests at their most observant and appreciative of the food, not yet distracted by conversation, and, possibly, by a fair amount of good wine. First courses and puddings can both be inspiring because there is a chance for a bit of fantasy and artistry. And like puddings, since they are not absolutely essential, they seem more of a treat. If you are a true vegetarian, you could combine starters and vegetable side dishes to
make a complete one-course main meal. Alternatively, just two could be used for a light meal served simply with good bread – possibly one from the breads chapter. A first course must never be too filling; it is, after all, supposed to titillate the appetite for further good things. You should always choose something which has not only quite different ingredients to the main course, but contrasting colour and texture too. Soups are always popular and look particularly special presented in a handsome tureen.

Fresh plum tomato and basil tart with olive oil and garlic crust

The crust of this summer tart is very simple to make. It can be baked blind without weighting down, it retains its shape well while cooking, and it is still wonderfully crisp when filled. Try and use deep red plum tomatoes because their flavour is best for cooking.

For the crust:
 175g (6oz) plain flour
 1 teaspoon salt
 2 large garlic cloves, chopped finely
 5 tablespoons extra virgin olive oil
 1 tablespoon water
For the filling:
 1kg (2lb) fresh plum tomatoes
 2 tablespoons extra virgin olive oil
 3–4 large garlic cloves, sliced thinly
 2 teaspoons caster sugar
 25g (1oz) butter
 12 fresh basil leaves, sliced thinly
 6–8 fresh sage leaves (optional)
 Salt and black pepper
 Fresh basil and sage leaves, to
  garnish (optional)

◀ *Fresh plum tomato and basil tart with olive oil and garlic crust*

To make the crust, set the oven to preheat at Gas Mark 6/200°C/400°F. Sift the flour and salt into a bowl. Put the garlic into a saucepan with the olive oil and place the pan over a medium heat for about two minutes. Remove the pan from the heat and stir in the water. Pour this hot mixture gradually into the flour, stirring it with a wooden spoon to form a dough. Then, using your fingers, press pieces of the dough firmly and evenly to the sides and base of an ungreased 24cm (9½-inch) diameter, loose-bottomed flan tin. Prick the base lightly all over with a fork and refrigerate for about 20 minutes. Bake the crust in the centre of the oven for about 25 minutes or until the crust is crisp in the centre.

While the crust is cooking, make the filling. Put the tomatoes into a bowl, pour boiling water over them and leave them for a few minutes. Drain and peel the tomatoes. Slice each tomato into six or eight slices, depending on size. Put the olive oil into a fairly large, heavy-based saucepan over a medium heat. Add the sliced tomatoes and

garlic and cook, stirring often, for about 20 minutes until you have a soft thick mixture. If the tomatoes produce a lot of juice, bubble the mixture at the end to reduce it. Then add the caster sugar and butter and stir for a few minutes. Remove the pan from the heat and season the mixture to taste with salt and plenty of black pepper. Stir the basil into the tomato mixture. When the crust is ready (if it is ready before the filling, just keep it warm in a low oven) spoon the tomato mixture evenly into it. If you are using the sage leaves, heat about two tablespoons of olive oil in a frying pan over a fairly high heat. Add the sage leaves and toss them around for a few minutes just until they are crisp but not burnt. Put them on to the centre of the tart. Put the tart on top of a tin or jam jar and push down the sides. Then, using a spatula, carefully ease the tart off the base of the tin on to a large flat serving plate.
TO SERVE Serve the tart hot or just warm, garnished with the fresh sage and basil leaves, if liked.
Serves 6

SHALLOT AND SPRING ONION TART WITH CRUNCHY HOT BUTTER PASTRY

This lovely tart can also be served with salad for a light meal. The pastry is easy and does not need to be baked blind.

FOR THE PASTRY:
  125g (4oz) plain flour
  125g (4oz) semolina or ground rice
  1 teaspoon salt
  125g (4oz) butter
  1 tablespoon water
  1 egg white
FOR THE FILLING:
  750g (1½lb) shallots
  2 tablespoons olive oil
  1 bunch of spring onions
  1 large egg
  2 egg yolks
  150ml (¼ pint) double cream
  2 teaspoons caster sugar
  Salt and black pepper

Mix the flour, semolina and the salt together in a bowl. Gently melt the butter with the water in a small saucepan. Pour the hot butter on to the flour, stirring it in until you have a warm dough. Press pieces of the dough over the bottom and up the sides of an ungreased 25cm (10-inch) loose-bottomed fluted flan tin, bringing the edge slightly up above the rim of the tin. Brush the pastry case all over with egg white and refrigerate while you prepare the filling.

Peel the shallots and slice them across in fairly thin rings. Put the olive oil into a large heavy frying pan over a medium heat. Add the shallots and cook, stirring often, for about 15 minutes or until the shallots are really soft. If they begin to brown, reduce the heat. Then leave the shallots on one side to cool a bit.

Set the oven to preheat at Gas Mark 7/220°C/425°F. Prepare the spring onions and slice them into 5mm (¼-inch) pieces, using as much of the green part as possible. Whisk the egg and egg yolks together in a bowl and then whisk in the cream. Season with salt and plenty of black pepper.

Stir the cooled shallots and the spring onions into the egg and cream mixture. Pour the mixture into the pastry case. Level the surface of the tart and sprinkle with the caster sugar. Cook the tart towards the top of the preheated oven for about 25 minutes or until the tart is just set in the middle and small speckles of black have appeared on the surface. Put the flan tin on to a tin or jam jar and push the sides down carefully. As the pastry is very crumbly, you may find it easiest to place the tart on to a serving plate still on its tin base, although if you leave it to cool a bit and use a thin spatula, you can carefully ease the pastry off.
Serves 8

SUMMER STUFFED ONIONS WITH FRESH MINT, DILL AND PARMESAN CHEESE

With a fresh, herby sauce enveloping the chopped onion and petits pois in the centre of a soft half-onion shell, these stuffed onions make an appetizing cold first course. You can use other tender fresh herbs in the sauce, or you can use feta cheese instead of Parmesan. Don't chill this dish before serving because the flavour is best at room temperature.

  3 large Spanish onions
  175g (6oz) frozen petits pois
  1 large garlic clove, sliced roughly
  75g (3oz) mixed fresh mint and dill
  *15g (½oz) freshly grated Parmesan
    cheese*
  4 tablespoons lemon juice
  150ml (¼ pint) extra virgin olive oil
  2 teaspoons caster sugar
  *25g (1oz) pine kernels, toasted
    (optional)*
  *Whole sprigs of mint and dill, to
    decorate*
  Salt and black pepper

Set the oven to preheat at Gas Mark 6/200°C/400°F. Place the whole unpeeled onions in a roasting pan and cook them on the centre shelf for 45–50 minutes. Remove the pan and leave the onions to cool. Meanwhile, cook the petits pois, drain them and leave them on one side. Put the garlic into a food processor with the fresh mint and dill, the Parmesan, the lemon juice, the olive oil and the sugar. Whizz until the sauce is as smooth as possible; then season the sauce to taste with a little salt and black pepper.

When the onions are cold, cut off the top and bottom of each and peel off the skin. Slice the onions in half, crossways, and with a spoon, take out all the soft inside of each onion, leaving the outer shell. Brush the outside with oil. Chop the inside part of the onions into small pieces. Place in a bowl and stir in the pine kernels (if using), petits pois and the sauce.
TO SERVE Place the onion shells on six individual plates and spoon in the onion, pea and herb mixture, piling it up in the centre. Decorate with sprigs of fresh mint and dill. Then spoon a little more olive oil over the top of each onion before serving.
Serves 6

▲ *Summer stuffed onions with fresh mint, dill and Parmesan cheese*

◄ *Shallot and spring onion tart with crunchy hot butter pastry*

SUKIE'S SYMPHONY

I made this mixture of briefly steamed squid with ribbons of pink trout on a salsa-type sauce especially for my great friend Sukie. It is a cold dish which you can serve as a first course or a main course.

75–125g (3–4oz) small leaf
    spinach
4 tablespoons lemon juice
1 small aubergine
175g (6oz) plum tomatoes
3 tablespoons extra virgin olive oil
125g (4oz) ready-prepared small
    squid
125g (4oz) pink trout fillets
1 tablespoon sherry vinegar
½ teaspoon caster sugar
Generous bunch of dill, chopped
    finely
Salt and black pepper

Boil the spinach for about one minute. Drain well. Put the lemon juice into a jug, and make it up to 450ml (¾ pint) with water. Pour the liquid into a saucepan. Peel the aubergine and cut the flesh into small cubes, throwing the cubes into the lemon water as you go to prevent them from becoming discoloured. Cover the saucepan and bring the liquid to the boil. Cook the aubergines for 5–8 minutes or until they are soft and translucent. Drain the aubergines. Put the tomatoes in a bowl and cover with boiling water, then peel them and slice the flesh.

Heat two tablespoons of the extra virgin olive oil in a large saucepan over a medium heat. Add the tomato and cook for one minute. Then add the cooked aubergines and remove the pan from the heat.

Slice the squid across thinly, leaving the tentacles whole. Skin the trout fillets and slice lengthways thinly. Put the squid and trout into the top of a steamer. Steam the fish for about two minutes only, just until the squid is opaque and the trout is a pale pink. Remove the fish from the heat and leave it to one side to cool. Add the sherry vinegar and caster sugar to the vegetable mixture in the pan. Stir in the remaining olive oil and season the mixture with salt and black pepper. Stir in the chopped dill. Finally, roughly mix in the wilted spinach leaves.

Spoon this mixture into a shallow serving dish and arrange the tangle of squid and trout on top of the sauce. Whether a first or main course, this should be served at room temperature.
Serves 4 as a starter

PRAWN AND SMOKED HADDOCK MOUSSE WITH SCALLOP SAUCE

This pretty, melt-in-the-mouth mousse can also be served as a main course for four people.

For the mousse:
    300ml (½ pint) double cream
    Generous pinch of saffron strands
    1–2 fresh red chillies
    250g (8oz) cooked, peeled prawns
    500g (1lb) smoked haddock,
        chopped roughly
    4 large egg whites
    2 egg yolks
    2–3 pinches of chilli powder
    Salt
For the sauce:
    6 fresh scallops
    75g (3oz) unsalted butter
    1 tablespoon cornflour
    300ml (½ pint) milk
    2 egg yolks, whisked lightly
    2.5–5cm (1–2-inch) piece of fresh
        root ginger, sliced very thinly
    Generous handful of fresh coriander
        leaves, chopped roughly
    3–4 teaspoons sherry vinegar
    Chilli powder
    Salt
    Sprig of fresh coriander, to garnish

To make the mousse, put the cream and saffron into a saucepan. Bring the mixture to boiling point, then stir and leave to cool, stirring now and then to infuse the saffron. Meanwhile, cut the chilli in half lengthways under running water and remove the seeds and stem. Slice the chilli across very thinly. Generously butter a cake tin big enough to take 1 litre (1¾ pints) of liquid. Arrange a few prawns in the centre of the cake tin base with one or two slivers of chilli among them. When the cream has cooled, put the chopped haddock into a food processor with the egg whites and two egg yolks. Whizz the mixture until just puréed. Then turn it into a mixing bowl, add the saffron cream and the remaining prawns and stir to mix thoroughly. Season with the chilli powder to taste, and salt if you think it needs it.

Put a roasting tin full of hot water on the centre shelf of the oven and heat to Gas Mark 4/180°C/350°F. Spoon the mousse mixture into the cake tin and spread level. Put the cake tin into the roasting tin of water and cook for 25–30 minutes or until firm to touch.

While the mousse is cooking, make the sauce. Slice the white part of each scallop and cut the corals in half, unless they are very small. Melt 25g (1oz) of the butter in a heavy-based saucepan, then remove the pan from the heat, and using a wooden spoon, stir in the cornflour until smooth. Gradually stir in the milk. Put the pan back over the heat and bring to the boil, stirring. Allow the mixture to bubble for 2–3 minutes, stirring all the time, until it is thickened and smooth. Then add the whisked egg yolks and the scallops and ginger to the sauce. Bubble gently, stirring for a further minute or two, until the scallops are opaque. Remove the pan from the heat. Stir in the coriander. Add the sherry vinegar, chilli powder and salt to taste.
TO SERVE Loosen the edges of the mousse carefully with a knife and turn it out on to a warmed serving plate. Garnish with a sprig of coriander. Pour the sauce into a warmed bowl.
Serves 6

▶ *Sukie's symphony; prawn and smoked haddock mousse with scallop sauce*

AVOCADOS IN SPINACH JELLY WITH GARLIC AND CHILLI

This is a refreshingly different way to serve avocado, and it won't discolour even if prepared ahead. Try to buy firm avocados so they retain their shape.

> 450ml (¾ pint) water
> 3–4 pinches of chilli powder
> 5 spinach leaves, chopped roughly
> 3 garlic cloves, chopped roughly
> 4 teaspoons caster sugar
> 3 avocados
> 2 tablespoons white wine vinegar
> Juice of 1 lemon
> 3 teaspoons powdered gelatine or
>   3 tablespoons agar-agar flakes
> 1–2 sprigs of fresh dill (optional), to
>   garnish
> Salt

Put the water, chilli powder, chopped spinach, garlic, sugar and a good sprinkling of salt into a saucepan. Bring the mixture to the boil, then simmer gently for about 10 minutes.

Meanwhile, cut the avocados in half lengthways. Remove the stones and peel off the skin, taking as much care as possible not to spoil the shape of the avocado by pressing into the flesh. Cut the avocado flesh across in fairly thin, half-moon slices and put the slices into a bowl, sprinkling them with the white wine vinegar as you do so to prevent them from discolouring. Then arrange the avocado slices in layers in an attractive 1.2-litre (2-pint) serving dish.

Remove the spinach mixture from the heat and sprinkle in the gelatine or agar-agar flakes. Ensure that it has thoroughly dissolved, referring to the instructions on the packet if necessary. Stir in the lemon juice.

Strain the liquid only through a fine strainer into a jug, discarding any spinach and garlic left in the strainer. Immediately pour the strained liquid on to the avocados, slowly so that it seeps right through down to the bottom of the serving dish and between all the slices of avocado. Leave the jelly until cool. Refrigerate the jelly for at least three hours, or until set. Take out of the refrigerator just before serving. Garnish with the fresh dill, if using.
Serves 6

NEW POTATOES WITH QUAILS' EGGS AND HERBY CREAM CHEESE MAYONNAISE

Potatoes are one of my favourite ingredients and I quite often use them in a first course dish. The cream cheese mayonnaise is not a mayonnaise in the true sense of the word because it uses no eggs; the light creaminess combined with fresh basil, parsley, extra virgin olive oil and hazelnut oil is lovely. If quails' eggs are not available, use small hens' eggs.

> 500g (1lb) small waxy new potatoes,
>   unpeeled
> 12 quails' eggs (or 6 small hens'
>   eggs, size 5)
> A few leaves of flat leaf parsley, to
>   garnish
> *FOR THE MAYONNAISE:*
>   Handful of flat leaf parsley
>   14 fresh basil leaves
>   (approximately)
>   125g (4oz) full-fat soft cheese
>   2 tablespoons lemon juice
>   5 tablespoons extra virgin olive oil
>   3 tablespoons hazelnut oil
>   Salt
>   Chilli powder

◀ *Avocados in spinach jelly with garlic and chilli*

Steam or boil the potatoes until they are cooked, then leave on one side. Lower the eggs gently into the boiling water, bring the water back to the boil again and boil for 2½–3 minutes (or 6 minutes for hens' eggs). Drain and put the eggs in cold water to cool.

To make the mayonnaise, reserve a few perfect leaves of flat leaf parsley for garnishing later and chop the remaining parsley and basil leaves roughly. Put the full-fat soft cheese into a food processor with one tablespoon of the lemon juice and whizz together. Then add the olive and hazelnut oils, a very little of each at a time, whizzing well between each addition. Whizz in the remaining tablespoon of lemon juice, season to taste with salt and chilli powder and then whizz in the chopped parsley and basil. If you are not eating this dish immediately, refrigerate the mayonnaise until it is needed.

TO SERVE Shortly before eating, assemble the dish. Peel the eggs and slice both the eggs and potatoes in half lengthways. Arrange the potatoes and eggs together on individual serving plates and spoon some of the herby cream cheese mayonnaise to one side. Garnish the dish with the reserved whole parsley leaves.
Serves 4

▲ *New potatoes with quails' eggs and herby cream cheese mayonnaise*

PICKLED HERRING AND APPLE IN SOURED CREAM

Try to find herring fillets marinated in a mild, sweet brine for this quick-to-make refreshing first course.

4 pickled herring fillets
1 large firm dessert apple
300ml (½ pint) soured cream
½ whole nutmeg, grated
1 small red onion, sliced thinly
1 handful of fresh coriander leaves
1 generous handful of fresh mint
* leaves, chopped finely*
1 pretty-leaved lettuce
Salt
Chilli powder

Rinse the herring fillets thoroughly under running cold water and pat them dry with kitchen paper. Using a sharp knife, cut the fillets across into thin pieces. Peel the apple, cut it in half, then slice it in very thin half-moon slices. Spoon the soured cream into a mixing bowl and add the grated nutmeg. Season with salt and chilli powder to taste, then stir in the sliced herring, the onion and the apple. Reserve a few perfect whole leaves of coriander for garnish and roughly chop up the rest. Stir the chopped mint and coriander leaves into the soured cream

mixture. Cover the bowl and leave it in the refrigerator until you are ready to assemble the dish to eat.

Shortly before serving, arrange some pretty lettuce leaves on six individual serving plates. Spoon the herring and soured cream mixture in a pile in the centre of each plate.
TO SERVE A perfect accompaniment to this dish is Highland Oatcakes (page 148); otherwise serve with the thinnest slices of brown bread or German rye bread. Garnish with the whole coriander leaves.
Serves 6

SMOKED SALMON IN PRAWN CREAM WITH DILL AND GREEN PEPPERCORNS

This mixture is creamy, though no cream is used, and more delicate than a pâté.

50g (2oz) unsalted butter
250g (8oz) peeled prawns
150ml (¼ pint) Greek-style yogurt
¼ whole nutmeg, grated
250g (8oz) smoked salmon
2 teaspoons green peppercorns
Handful of fresh dill, chopped finely
2–4 pinches of chilli powder
Salt

Melt the butter gently in a small saucepan. Pour the butter into a food processor with the prawns and the yogurt. Whizz thoroughly until smooth. Turn the mixture into a mixing bowl and season to taste with the grated nutmeg and chilli powder and a little salt. Slice the salmon up into small pieces. Put four rounded teaspoons of the salmon pieces on one side, and cover with clingfilm. Stir the remaining salmon into the puréed

prawn mixture. Spoon the prawn mixture into six cocotte dishes or little bowls and chill for several hours in the refrigerator. Before serving, chop the peppercorns finely, mix them with the dill and sprinkle them all over the top of each dish. Lastly, scatter the reserved smoked salmon pieces over each dish and serve.
TO SERVE Accompany with thin slivers of toast.
Serves 6

PINK TROUT BALLS WITH DILL VINAIGRETTE

This light dish makes a titillating start to a summer meal.

FOR THE TROUT BALLS:
250–300g (8–10oz) pink trout
* fillets, skinned*
3–4 pinches of chilli powder
Finely grated zest of 1 small lemon
2 tablespoons crème fraîche
1 large egg white (size 1)
1 small frisée lettuce
Salt
Fresh dill, to garnish
FOR THE DILL AND LEMON VINAIGRETTE:
4 tablespoons lemon juice
1 teaspoon caster sugar
Small bunch of dill, chopped finely
175ml (6 fl oz) light olive oil
Sea salt and black pepper

Put the trout into a food processor with the chilli powder, lemon zest, crème fraîche and egg white. Sprinkle with a little salt and whizz until smooth. Turn the mixture into a bowl, cover and refrigerate for about 30 minutes. Then, using dampened hands, take up small amounts of the mixture and roll into balls about the size of a large marble. Bring a large saucepan of salted water to a fierce boil, drop in the balls separately and boil them for 2–3 minutes or until they all rise to the surface. Remove the saucepan from the heat. Using a slotted spoon, remove the balls carefully, putting them into a bowl on one side to cool. Do not refrigerate.

Meanwhile make the vinaigrette. Put the lemon juice and caster sugar

into a clean 500g (1lb) jar. Add a little crushed sea salt and black pepper, to taste. Next add the dill and olive oil, cover the jar with a tight-fitting lid and shake the vinaigrette thoroughly. Taste for seasoning and add a little more lemon juice if you like.
TO SERVE Lay the frisée leaves on four individual plates. Arrange the fish balls among the tangle of leaves. Just before serving, shake up the dressing again and spoon a little over each plate. Garnish with fresh dill.
Serves 4

▶ *Pickled herring and apple in soured cream; smoked salmon in prawn cream with dill and green peppercorns; pink trout balls with dill vinaigrette*

FRESH TOMATO SOUP WITH DICED COURGETTES, BASIL LEAVES AND OLIVE OIL

There are few dishes as good as a light and refreshing tomato soup. You can make the soup in advance but add the courgettes only a few minutes before serving. For a completely vegetarian dish, this soup is still excellent without the anchovies.

1.1kg (2½lb) ripe tomatoes
50g (2oz) butter
50g (2oz) can of anchovy fillets
4 garlic cloves, chopped finely
3 teaspoons caster sugar
1.2 litres (2 pints) vegetable stock
500g (1lb) courgettes
Extra virgin olive oil
10–14 fresh basil leaves, sliced thinly
Salt and black pepper

Slit the tops of the tomatoes and put them into a bowl. Pour over enough boiling water to cover and leave them for 1–2 minutes. Then skin the tomatoes, chop the flesh finely and leave on one side.

Put the butter into a large, heavy saucepan, add the anchovies and their oil and put the pan over a low heat. Stir the mixture until the anchovies dissolve into a purée. Then add the chopped tomatoes and garlic, the caster sugar and the vegetable stock. (If your tomatoes are not really ripe and deep red, you can add a little tomato purée or sun-dried tomato paste.) Bring the mixture up to the boil and then simmer gently in the open pan, stirring often, for 20–30 minutes until the tomatoes

are completely mushy. Season the soup to taste with black pepper, and salt only if necessary. Put the soup on one side until the meal is nearly ready.

Cut the courgettes into small cubes. To reheat the soup, bring it up to boiling point, add the cubed courgettes and allow the soup to bubble for 1–2 minutes until they are just tender.
TO SERVE Ladle the soup into individual bowls, then add one or two tablespoons of extra virgin olive oil to each bowl and sprinkle the fresh, sliced basil leaves on top. Serve the soup with a plate of thin shavings of fresh Parmesan cheese (you can use a potato peeler for this) and warmed Italian ciabatta bread or rolls.
Serves 6–8

SPICED AUBERGINE AND MINT SOUP WITH CUCUMBER

This is a chilled soup which, for me, is evocative of my young childhood days in the Middle East. The smoky richness of the grilled aubergines is combined with characteristic spices, yogurt and mint – all irresistible flavours. If possible, buy the spices whole and grind them in a coffee grinder shortly before using.

2 large or 3 medium aubergines
3 tablespoons olive oil
5 large garlic cloves, halved lengthways
1 rounded teaspoon ground cumin
1 rounded teaspoon ground coriander
1 rounded teaspoon paprika
4 tablespoons lemon juice
2 rounded teaspoons caster sugar
Generous handful of fresh mint leaves
600ml (1 pint) natural yogurt
1 cucumber, peeled and cubed
Salt
3–5 pinches of chilli powder
Single cream, to serve
Mint leaves, to garnish

◄ *Fresh tomato soup with diced courgettes, basil leaves and olive oil*

Put the aubergines under the hottest grill for about 10–20 minutes, turning them once or twice until the skins are really blackened and even cracked.

Meanwhile, put the olive oil in a frying pan over a low heat. Add the halved cloves of garlic and the ground spices and stir just until the garlic has softened – keep the heat low so that it doesn't burn.

Dip the charred aubergines in a sink of cold water so they are cool enough to handle. Scrape out all the flesh of the aubergines into a strainer. Press out as much liquid from the aubergine flesh as you can, using the back of a spoon. Then put the flesh into a food processor with the lemon juice and whizz to a smooth purée.

Add the fried garlic with its oil and spices, the caster sugar and the mint leaves to the purée in the food processor. Whizz until the mint is very finely chopped. Turn the mixture into a mixing bowl and stir in the yogurt. Season to taste with salt and chilli powder. Stir the peeled, cubed cucumber into the aubergine soup. Put the bowl in the refrigerator to chill well for about half an hour.

TO SERVE Serve in individual bowls with a generous swirl of single cream and a small fresh mint leaf to decorate each one.
Serves 6

▲ *Spiced aubergine and mint soup with cucumber*

EMERALD SOUP WITH SCALLOPS AND WATER CHESTNUTS

For a clear scarlet soup, substitute finely chopped raw beetroot for the spinach.

500g (1lb) spinach
1.75 litres (3 pints) water
5cm (2-inch) piece of fresh root
  ginger
4 whole star anise
Coarsely grated zest and strained
  juice of 1 orange
2 tablespoons white wine vinegar
375–500g (12oz – 1lb) queen
  scallops or 8–10 large ones
1 bunch of spring onions
227g (7½oz) can of water chestnuts
Salt and black pepper

Remove any thick stems from the spinach. Roughly chop the leaves, then put the spinach, the water and about three teaspoons of salt into a large pan. Cut up the ginger fairly roughly without peeling and add it to the pan, together with the star anise and the orange zest and strained juice. Bring the mixture to the boil, then cover the pan and simmer gently for 15–20 minutes. Remove the pan from the heat and strain the liquid through a fine strainer into a bowl, pressing the spinach down hard with the back of a wooden spoon to extract all its liquid. Pour the strained liquid back through the strainer into a clean pan. Add the vinegar, season to taste with salt and pepper and leave the pan to one side.

Leave queen scallops whole, but slice larger scallops across thinly and then cut the orange coral across into 2–3 pieces. Slice the spring onions into 5mm (¼-inch) pieces, using as much of the green part as possible. Drain the water chestnuts and slice them very thinly. If you aren't going to eat this soup for several hours, put the scallops, spring onions and water chestnuts into the refrigerator and cover them with clingfilm. Just before serving, bring the saucepan of spinach liquid up to the boil, then reduce the heat so that it is barely bubbling and add the scallops, spring onions and water chestnuts. Cook gently for only two minutes, or just until the scallops are opaque.
TO SERVE Serve immediately from a tureen with crusty rolls or bread.
Serves 6

CHILLED COURGETTE, AVOCADO AND YOGURT SOUP

Here is a tangy, refreshing and easily made soup for lazy summer meals.

1 fresh red chilli
900ml (1½ pints) chicken or
  vegetable stock
500g (1lb) small courgettes, cubed
1 large ripe avocado
4 tablespoons lemon juice
300ml (½ pint) Greek-style yogurt
Handful of fresh mint leaves, sliced
  across in thin strips
Salt and black pepper

Cut the chilli open lengthways under cold running water and remove the seeds and stem, then chop the flesh finely. Bring the chicken or vegetable stock to the boil in a saucepan, then add the courgettes and the chilli. Cover the pan and simmer for just about three minutes, or until the courgettes are slightly softened but still a bright green. Remove the pan from the heat and, using a slotted spoon, remove the courgette pieces from the stock and put them on one side. Now, cut the avocado in half, remove the stone and scoop out the flesh into a food processor with the lemon juice, yogurt and a little of the stock. Whizz until smooth, then spoon this purée into the pan with the remaining stock and stir to mix evenly. Season to taste with some salt and black pepper and leave until cold. Stir in the courgettes and the mint. Pour the mixture into a serving bowl and chill well in the refrigerator before serving.
Serves 6

BUTTER BEAN SOUP WITH GRILLED PEPPERS AND SAUTÉED GARLIC

300g (10oz) dried butter beans
1 large or 2 small red peppers
40g (1½oz) unsalted butter
600ml (1 pint) milk
2 tablespoons extra virgin olive oil
2–3 large garlic cloves, sliced thinly
2 tablespoons lemon juice
2–4 pinches of chilli powder
Salt

◄ *Emerald soup with scallops and water chestnuts; chilled courgette, avocado and yogurt soup; butter bean soup with grilled peppers and sautéed garlic*

Soak the butter beans in cold water for several hours or overnight. Drain the beans, cover them in fresh unsalted water and simmer gently in a covered pan until they become very soft – about 30 minutes to one hour. Meanwhile, quarter the pepper lengthways (or cut into halves if using smaller peppers), discarding the seeds and stem. Lay the pieces skin side upwards under a very hot grill until they are completely blackened. Place them in a plastic or paper bag until they have cooled slightly, then remove the black skin and cut the peppers into very thin strips. Drain the cooked butter beans, then purée in a food processor together with the butter. Gradually whizz in the milk and then add chilli powder and a little salt to taste. Put the oil into a large saucepan over a fairly high heat, add the garlic and stir for a few minutes until the garlic turns golden brown, but is not burnt. Add the soup to the saucepan and heat. Finally, stir in the lemon juice gradually and add the strips of grilled pepper.
Serves 4–5

PASTA, GRAINS & PULSES

Grains and pulses are invaluable for giving body and protein to a vegetarian meal, but they are too often abused, with the result that they become stodgy, monotone and formless. This need not be the case, as I hope to prove in this chapter. Combined with carefully cooked vegetables or with chicken and fish you can create something really exciting. For years I found rice extremely boring, but that was before I had experienced the light fluffiness and real flavour of Persian rice, the delicate nuttiness of basmati and Thai fragrant rice and the irresistible texture of a risotto made with arborio rice. Luckily, these kinds of rice are now much more easily available as are many more exotic ingredients and aromatics to combine with them. Dried beans are versatile and satisfying, but age and condition greatly affect their cooking time, so they have to be checked fairly often. Their protein content is a particular bonus for vegetarians, and for me they are the ultimate comfort food. Pasta is, of course, almost everyone's favourite, and invariably the answer when you have to produce a last-minute meal. It is such a good and versatile vehicle for other ingredients that there is endless scope for experimenting with Italian or more exotic flavours.

BROAD BEAN, ONION AND SAFFRON RISOTTO

Before I had tasted a real risotto, I had no idea of its wonderfully smooth creaminess and subtle texture. It relies not only on the rice, which should be the Italian arborio or similar variety, but also on a really fine homemade stock. Whenever I have made chicken stock, I make risotto. For vegetarians, a good fresh vegetable stock is also successful.

*1.5 litres (2½ pints) homemade
  chicken or vegetable stock
Generous pinch of saffron strands
65g (2½oz) unsalted butter
4 tablespoons olive oil
2 large onions, chopped
5 large garlic cloves, chopped finely
500g (1lb) risotto rice
500g (1lb) frozen baby broad beans
Salt and black pepper*

◀ *Broad bean, onion and saffron risotto*

Put the chicken or vegetable stock into a saucepan, add the saffron and bring the stock to the boil. Remove the stock from the heat and leave it for at least 15 minutes, stirring occasionally to infuse the saffron. Put the stock over a low heat.

Melt 50g (2oz) of the butter with the olive oil in a large saucepan over a fairly low heat. Add the chopped onion and stir until the onion is soft and translucent, but not browned. Then add the chopped garlic and stir the mixture for one minute. Next add the rice and stir for about two minutes. Pour in about 150ml (¼ pint) of the hot stock and bring it to simmering point. Using a wooden spoon, stir the rice until it has absorbed the stock, then add a little more stock.

Continue like this, adding a little more stock each time the stock has been absorbed, stirring all the time. It will probably take about 30 minutes to cook the rice to the point where it is soft but still has a slight bite to it.

Shortly before all the stock has been added, bring a saucepan of salted water to the boil. Cook the broad beans for 2–3 minutes only and then drain through a strainer.

Add the broad beans to the risotto after you have added the last of the stock. Finally, stir in the remaining butter and season to taste with salt, if necessary, and plenty of black pepper. Turn the risotto into a heated serving dish and eat without delay.
TO SERVE Serve with a chunk of Parmesan cheese to grate freshly on to each serving. Risotto can be eaten simply on its own, or accompanied by a green salad if you wish.
Serves 6

SMOKED HADDOCK AND MUSHROOM LASAGNE WITH CRUNCHY ALMOND TOP

Lasagne is useful for large families or for parties as it can be prepared well ahead and then cooked when you are ready. Use fresh lasagne if available.

250g (8oz) oven-ready lasagne
* sheets or fresh lasagne*
500g (1lb) skinned smoked haddock
* fillets or other smoked white fish*
50g (2oz) butter
2 large garlic cloves, chopped finely
½ nutmeg, grated
50g (2oz) plain flour
300ml (½ pint) natural yogurt
900ml (1½ pints) milk
250g (8oz) grated cheese
10–12 sun-dried tomatoes, sliced
* thinly*
175g (6oz) chestnut mushrooms,
* sliced thinly*
Generous handful of parsley,
* chopped roughly*
75g (3oz) flaked almonds
Grated Parmesan, for sprinkling
Salt and black pepper

If you are using oven-ready lasagne, it cooks better if soaked for 10–15 minutes in a sink filled with hot water and a little oil. Then remove the sheets and lay them out separately on a clean cloth to drain. Steam the fish for 2–3 minutes only and leave on one side. Melt the butter in a fairly large saucepan over a medium heat. Add the garlic and the grated nutmeg and stir for 30 seconds. Remove the saucepan from the heat and stir in the flour until smooth. Then stir in the yogurt. Return the pan to the heat and stir in one direction only until the mixture starts to bubble. Now add the milk gradually, stirring all the time, and increase the heat until the mixture comes to the boil. Simmer the mixture, still stirring, for 2–3 minutes until it is slightly thickened. Then add the grated cheese and stir until the cheese has melted. Remove from the heat and season to taste, but do not add more salt if your fish is already salty.

Set the oven to preheat at Gas Mark 4/180°C/350°F. Pour a little more than 300ml (½ pint) of the cheese sauce into a measuring jug and reserve it for the top. Then flake the fish into the remaining sauce in the pan and stir in the prepared sun-dried tomatoes, mushrooms and parsley. Generously butter a large, ovenproof gratinée dish and arrange a layer of lasagne sheets on the bottom. Cover these with a layer of the sauce, then cover with another layer of the lasagne. Repeat this process, ending with a layer of lasagne. Then spread over the reserved cheese sauce and scatter the flaked almonds evenly on top. Finally, sprinkle the top liberally with grated Parmesan cheese.

When you are ready to cook, bake the lasagne on the centre shelf of the oven for 35–40 minutes or until the top is a rich golden brown.
TO SERVE This is best served with a simple salad or just as it is.
Serves 8

CANNELLONI STUFFED WITH SPINACH IN WHITE WINE AND GRUYÈRE SAUCE

Lighter than most cannelloni dishes, this is good as a main course or a starter, and can easily be prepared in advance.

1kg (2lb) spinach leaves
Finely grated zest and juice of
* 1 orange*
300ml (½ pint) of milk
10 strands of saffron
16 oven-ready cannelloni tubes
50g (2oz) butter
Large garlic clove, chopped finely
25g (1oz) plain flour
450ml (¾ pint) dry white wine or
* cider*
150g (5oz) Gruyère or Emmental
* cheese, grated coarsely*
2 egg yolks
4–5 pinches of chilli powder
Salt and black pepper

Either boil or steam the spinach leaves until they are just soft. Drain the spinach thoroughly and then press out all the excess moisture using double thicknesses of kitchen paper. Put the leaves into a bowl and stir in the orange zest and a sprinkling of salt and black pepper. Put the milk and saffron into a small saucepan. Bring the milk up to bubbling, remove from the heat and leave on one side, stirring now and then to infuse the saffron into the milk.

Meanwhile, fill the cannelloni tubes as follows: using your hands, roll bits of the spinach into sausages of the same length as the cannelloni tubes but thinner. Hold a cannelloni tube upright and insert the sausage of spinach into it, pressing it in gently with the end of a thin-handled wooden spoon if necessary. When all the tubes are filled, lay them out neatly in a rectangular ovenproof gratinée dish.

Set the oven to preheat at Gas Mark 5/190°C/375°F. Melt the butter in a saucepan over a medium heat. Add the chopped garlic and stir for 30 seconds. Remove the pan from the heat and stir in the flour until smooth. Now

gradually stir in the milk and saffron, the white wine or cider and the orange juice. Put the pan back over the heat and bring to the boil, stirring all the time. Stir for about three minutes, keeping it bubbling, until it has thickened to the consistency of double cream. Add all but two tablespoons of the grated cheese and stir until the cheese has melted. Then remove the pan from the heat and whisk in the egg yolks. Finally, season to taste with salt and chilli powder and pour the sauce all over the cannelloni in the dish. Sprinkle the top evenly with the reserved cheese. Cook the dish just above the centre shelf of the preheated oven for 35 minutes or until the top is a rich golden brown. Serve immediately.
Serves 4

▶ *Smoked haddock and mushroom*
lasagne with crunchy almond top;
cannelloni stuffed with spinach in white
wine and gruyère sauce

BASMATI RICE COOKED IN WHITE WINE AND SAFFRON WITH SALMON

This rice dish does not have the creaminess of a risotto, which should always be made with arborio or a similar type rice. But basmati, India's king of rice, has supreme flavour, texture and lightness. You can also use Thai fragrant rice for this recipe.

250g (8oz) basmati rice
2 generous pinches of saffron
* strands*
Generous 300ml (½ pint) dry or
* medium sweet white wine*
50g (2oz) butter
1.1kg (2½lb) piece salmon
* (unfilleted weight), filleted and*
* skinned*
1 bunch of fresh chives, chopped
Generous handful of fresh dill,
* chopped*
Generous handful of flat leaf
* parsley, chopped*
Sea salt
5–6 pinches of chilli powder

Put the rice into a sieve and wash thoroughly with running cold water. Then put the rice into a bowl with 600ml (1 pint) of cold salted water and soak for at least one hour.

Meanwhile, put the saffron strands into a separate bowl together with a generous sprinkling of sea salt and the chilli powder. Put the wine into a saucepan. Bring the wine up to boiling point and then pour it into the bowl with the saffron and seasoning. Leave the saffron for the same length of time as you soak the rice, stirring once or twice to infuse the saffron strands.

Put the butter in a saucepan and melt it over a medium heat. Drain the rice through a sieve and stir it into the butter in the pan. Then add the wine and saffron mixture. Bring the mixture up to bubbling, cover the pan immediately with a well-fitting lid and turn the heat down to as low as you possibly can. Cook the rice for 10–14

minutes, until it is tender but still has a slight bite to it.

While the rice is cooking, cook the salmon. If the rice is ready a bit before the fish, turn off the heat, put a cloth between the lid and the saucepan and leave it in a warm place. To cook the salmon, simply put it in the top of a covered steamer over boiling water for 5–10 minutes – it depends on the thickness of the fillet – until the salmon is lightly cooked but still grades to a slightly darker pink in the centre. Then flake the fish into a mixing bowl.

When the rice is ready, turn it into the mixing bowl with the salmon and, using a large fork, mix together thoroughly. Season if necessary with more salt and chilli powder. Stir in the chopped herbs.

TO SERVE Turn the rice into the warmed serving dish and serve at once with a green salad.
Serves 4–5

GARLIC AND GREEN LENTIL RISOTTO

In Gujurat, the staple dish is *kichri*, a mixture of rice and lentils, which was the original inspiration for kedgeree. Here I have combined an Italian-style risotto with lentils, and flavoured it with an Indian mixture of herbs and spices.

1.2–1.25 litres (2–2¼ pints) chicken
* or vegetable stock*
1–2 fresh red chillis
65g (2½oz) unsalted butter
8 large garlic cloves, sliced in half
* lengthways*
5cm (2-inch) piece of fresh root
* ginger, chopped finely*
4–5 cardamom pods, crushed lightly
2 teaspoons cumin seeds
275g (9oz) risotto rice (arborio)
125g (4oz) green or brown lentils,
* washed through in cold water*
Handful of fresh coriander leaves,
* chopped roughly*
Salt

◀ *Basmati rice cooked in white wine and saffron with salmon*

Bring the stock up to the boil in a saucepan, and allow it to simmer gently throughout the making of your risotto. Cut the chillies open under running water, discard the seeds and stem and slice very finely across.

Melt 50g (2oz) of the butter in a large, heavy-based saucepan over a low heat. Add the garlic and stir until the garlic is soft, translucent and golden brown. Stir in the chopped ginger, the sliced chillies, the crushed cardamom pods and the cumin seeds. Then add the rice and lentils and stir for about two minutes. Next pour in about 150ml (¼ pint) of the simmering stock and stir constantly with a wooden spoon over a medium heat until the rice and lentils have absorbed all the stock. Add a little more simmering stock and stir until it has also been absorbed.

Continue like this until the rice is soft but still has a slight bite to it. If all the stock has been absorbed before the rice is ready, you can add a little boiling water. Finally, stir in the

remaining butter and add salt if necessary. Serve on a warm serving dish, sprinkled with the coriander.
Serves 4

▲ *Garlic and green lentil risotto*

CABBAGE LEAVES STUFFED WITH RED BEANS AND HERBY TOMATOES

This simple dish is both aromatic and piquant – the scented flavour of rosemary contrasts with a bite of chilli and ginger. It can be served as a side dish or with good bread as a main course.

375g (12oz) dried red kidney beans
625–750g (1¼–1½lb) loosely packed green cabbage, separated into leaves
2 sprigs of fresh rosemary
250g (8oz) tomatoes
1cm (½-inch) piece of fresh root ginger, chopped finely
3 large garlic cloves, chopped finely
1 rounded teaspoon paprika
1 tablespoon tomato purée
1 large egg (size 1)
2 tablespoons lemon juice
150ml (¼ pint) chicken or vegetable stock
1 fresh red chilli
Sea salt
2–3 pinches of chilli powder

Soak the kidney beans in plenty of cold water for at least eight hours or overnight. Drain the beans. Put them in a saucepan and cover them with unsalted water. Boil the beans rapidly for 10 minutes, then reduce the heat and simmer gently until they are just soft but not so soft they break up. Drain the beans in a colander and rinse through with cold water to cool them. Put the beans into a mixing bowl. Bring a saucepan of salted water to the boil. Add the cabbage leaves and boil them for two minutes until they are limp. Drain and lay them out on a flat surface.

Set the oven to preheat at Gas Mark 4/180°C/350°F. Take the leaves off one of the rosemary sprigs and chop them finely. Put the tomatoes in a bowl and pour boiling water over to cover them. Leave the tomatoes for two minutes, then drain, skin and chop them. Add the tomatoes to the kidney beans together with the ginger, garlic, chopped rosemary, paprika and tomato purée. Season well with sea salt and chilli powder and mix thoroughly with a wooden spoon. Finally, whisk the egg lightly then stir it into the beans.

Butter a large shallow casserole dish. Spoon the bean mixture in compact piles on to each cabbage leaf and bring up the sides and then the ends like a parcel to enclose the beans completely. Carefully place the cabbage bundles, join side down, in the casserole. Pour the lemon juice and stock over them. Break the remaining sprig of rosemary into pieces and place them in the stock among the cabbage parcels. Cut the chilli open lengthways under running water, discard the seeds and stem and slice the flesh across very thinly. Scatter the chilli over the cabbage parcels and cover the casserole. Cook the dish in the centre of the oven for 45 minutes to one hour.
Serves 6

TOMATOES STUFFED WITH CRACKED WHEAT, PEAS AND CHUTNEY

These juicy stuffed tomatoes, packed with flavour, are delicious eaten either hot or cold as a first course or for a light meal, accompanied by crusty bread and a green salad, or they would also make good summer picnic fare. They are very simple and quick to prepare.

4 very large tomatoes
150g (5oz) cracked wheat (bulgar)
175g (6oz) frozen petits pois
3 tablespoons olive oil, plus a little extra for brushing
3 large garlic cloves, chopped very finely
1 small sprig of fresh rosemary, chopped very finely
2 rounded tablespoons tomato chutney
Generous handful of roughly chopped small mint leaves
Salt
Black pepper

◀ Cabbage leaves stuffed with red beans and herby tomatoes

Slice just the tops off the tomatoes and leave them to one side. Using a small spoon scoop out all the seeds and most of the flesh and chop the flesh into small pieces. Lightly salt the insides of the tomato shells and lay them upside down in a colander to drain away the excess liquid. Put the cracked wheat into a bowl and cover with water. Put the frozen petits pois in a strainer and rinse with cold water just to thaw them.

Put the oil into a large frying pan over a fairly high heat and add the chopped tomato, garlic and rosemary. Allow the mixture to bubble, stirring all the time, for about five minutes until well-reduced and thickened. Remove the pan from the heat and stir in the chutney. Drain the cracked wheat through a sieve and press out any excess moisture. Then stir the wheat into the tomato mixture together with the mint and peas. Season to taste with salt and black pepper.

Rinse the salt from the tomato shells and dry them with kitchen paper. Put the shells into a shallow ovenproof dish. Spoon the cracked wheat and pea mixture into the tomato shells and then balance the reserved tomato lids on top. Brush the tomatoes all over with olive oil. Cook the tomatoes on the centre shelf of a preheated oven, Gas Mark 4/180°C/350°F for 20–30 minutes, or until they are soft.
Serves 4

▲ Tomatoes stuffed with cracked wheat, peas and chutney

PASTA SHELLS WITH SMOKED OYSTERS AND QUICK-FRIED SPINACH

This simple, instant supper dish is nevertheless excellent. You can use smoked mussels instead of oysters, or a mixture of both. If you have one, a wok is better for this recipe than a frying pan.

375g (12oz) small spinach leaves
2 x 105g (3oz) cans of smoked
 oysters or smoked mussels
250–300g (8–10oz) pasta shells
125ml (4 fl oz) extra virgin olive oil
3 large garlic cloves, chopped finely
Salt and black pepper
Grated Parmesan, to serve
 (optional)

First prepare the ingredients. Wash and drain the spinach and then shake it in a cloth to dry it as much as possible. Then, if necessary, take the stalks off the spinach and cut up the leaves, unless they are really small. Open the cans of oysters so that they are ready to use. Then bring a large pan of salted water to boil, drop in the pasta shells and cook them for 7–12 minutes until they are *al dente* – just cooked but still with a very slight bite to them. As soon as you have put the water on to boil, you should start cooking the other ingredients. Put the olive oil into a

large, deep frying pan over a high heat. When the oil is very hot, add the garlic, followed by the spinach. Stir swiftly for barely one minute, just until the spinach has become limp. Lastly, stir in the smoked oysters and their oil. Remove the pan from the heat and season with plenty of black pepper and a little salt if needed. When the pasta is ready, drain and put the pasta into a heated serving bowl. Pour the frying pan mixture on top and lightly mix in the pasta. Serve immediately, with grated Parmesan, if liked.
Serves 4

CHICKEN AND SPINACH PASTA PIE

A pasta pie has two main advantages: not only is it a dish that can be put together quickly at the last minute, but it can also be prepared ahead of time to avoid any last-minute panics. Pasta is supremely popular, as is chicken, so a combination of the two is always a perfect family dish. This pasta pie can simply be cooked and then reheated, or it can be left in the refrigerator after you have spooned the sauce on top and sprinkled with grated cheese until you are ready to cook it. When you can find them, the extra-wide flat ribbon noodles are especially good for this dish, but the ordinary tagliatelle is also suitable.

500g (1lb) spinach leaves
125g (4oz) wide noodles (tagliatelle
 or wider)
500g–625g (1–1¼lb) boneless,
 skinless chicken thighs
2 tablespoons olive oil
2 large garlic cloves, chopped finely
1 rounded tablespoon tomato purée
3–4 pinches of chilli powder
25g (1oz) butter
2 rounded teaspoons ground mace
25g (1oz) plain flour
600ml (1 pint) milk
75g (3oz) grated Cheddar cheese
Salt and black pepper

◀ *Pasta shells with smoked oysters and quick-fried spinach*

Bring a saucepan of salted water to the boil, add the spinach and boil the leaves for only a few minutes or until they are just limp. Drain the spinach and press out all the excess moisture using the back of a spoon. Leave it to one side. Bring a large saucepan of salted water to the boil, add the pasta and cook it until the pasta is *al dente*. Drain the pasta and mix in a very little olive oil to prevent it sticking together. Keep the pasta in a bowl on one side.

Using a sharp knife, cut the chicken up into very small pieces. Put the olive oil into a large heavy frying pan over a fairly high heat. Add the chicken pieces and stir for 2–3 minutes, then add the chopped garlic and the tomato purée. Turn the heat down a little and continue stirring for a further three minutes. Remove the pan from the heat and season the chicken to taste with salt and the chilli powder. Then transfer the mixture to a large, shallow ovenproof dish and spread the top level. Cover the chicken evenly with the cooked spinach.

Set the oven to preheat to Gas Mark 6/200°C/400°F . Melt the butter in a saucepan. Stir in the mace and remove the pan from the heat. Then stir in the flour until the mixture is smooth. Gradually stir in the milk and return the pan to the heat. Bring the mixture to the boil, stirring all the time, and

then allow it to bubble, still stirring, for about three minutes until the sauce is thickened and smooth. Remove the pan from the heat and season to taste with salt and black pepper.

Pour half the sauce over the spinach in the dish. Then spread the cooked noodles over the sauce and spoon the remaining sauce on top. Finally, sprinkle the top with the grated Cheddar cheese. Cook the pie just above the centre of the preheated oven for 25–35 minutes or until it is a rich, golden brown.
TO SERVE Serve with a crisp green salad or a mixed salad.
Serves 6

▲ *Chicken and spinach pasta pie*

TAGLIATELLE WITH ROCKET, ORANGE ZEST AND HAZELNUT OIL

Rocket, orange zest and hazelnut oil is a perfect combination, making this one of the simplest, but most delicious, pastas.

Zest of 1 orange
250g (8oz) tagliatelle
4 tablespoons hazelnut oil
2 tablespoons extra virgin olive oil
3 generous handfuls of rocket leaves
Salt and black pepper

Put a serving bowl in a low oven to keep warm. Bring a large saucepan of salted water to the boil. Meanwhile, remove the zest from the orange in thin strips with a zester, or alternatively, grate the zest coarsely. When the water is boiling, add the tagliatelle and the orange zest and cook until the pasta is *al dente* – still with a slight bite to it. Drain the pasta and return it to the

empty saucepan. Stir in the hazelnut oil and olive oil. Season the pasta with salt and plenty of black pepper and lastly stir in the rocket leaves.

TO SERVE Turn the pasta into the warm serving bowl. Put a bowl of thinly shaved or freshly grated Parmesan cheese on the table to scatter on top of the pasta. Eat at once.
Serves 4

SPAGHETTI WITH PEAS, SPRING ONIONS AND PEA, MINT AND SMETANA SAUCE

A simple dish tasting of summer, this is perfect for a light lunch on a hot day. I find that the best fresh peas are those you know have only just been picked, as they become starchy within a day of picking. However, frozen petits pois work well for this recipe. You can use tagliatelle or other pasta instead of spaghetti.

500g (1lb) fresh peas or frozen
  petits pois
Generous handful of mint leaves
300ml (½ pint) creamed smetana
2 tablespoons extra virgin olive oil
1 bunch of spring onions
300g (10oz) spaghetti
Salt and black pepper
Fresh mint leaves, to garnish

Put the frozen petits pois into boiling salted water and boil for two minutes. If using fresh peas, boil for five minutes. Then drain the peas and put one-third of them into a food processor with the mint leaves, smetana and the olive oil. Whizz the mixture to a purée. Then put the mixture into a bowl and season to taste with salt and plenty of black pepper. Add the remaining peas and cover the bowl with foil. Put the sauce into a very low oven together with another bowl suitable for serving the pasta to keep warm while you are cooking the spaghetti.

Bring a large saucepan of salted water to the boil. While it is coming to the boil, slice the spring onions across into 5mm (¼-inch) pieces, using as

much of the green part as possible. When the water is boiling, put in the spaghetti and boil it for 7–10 minutes (perhaps less if you are using fresh pasta) or until it is *al dente* – cooked, but still with a slight bite to it. Drain the spaghetti into a colander and rinse with running hot water. Then put the spaghetti into the warmed serving bowl. Stir the spring onions into the sauce, then mix the sauce roughly into the pasta.

TO SERVE Garnish with fresh mint leaves and serve at once accompanied by a bowl of freshly grated Parmesan cheese or fine slivers of Parmesan shaved from a whole piece of cheese with a potato peeler.
Serves 4

SPAGHETTI WITH PECAN NUTS, PARSLEY, BASIL AND RED CHILLI

This pasta dish is quick and particularly delicious. It is perfect for a light supper. It is also very good made with chopped walnuts instead of pecans, but walnuts do have a rather stronger taste.

50g (2oz) shelled pecan nuts
1–2 large garlic cloves
2 red chillies
5 tablespoons extra virgin olive oil
Generous handful of flat-leaf
  parsley, chopped finely
3 tablespoons very hot water
10–14 leaves fresh basil, sliced
  thinly
250g (8oz) spaghetti
Salt

Put a serving bowl in a low oven to keep it warm. Put the pecan nuts into a food processor and grind them only roughly. Peel the garlic and chop it finely. Cut open the chillies under running water, remove the seeds and stem and then slice the chillies across very finely.

Put two tablespoons of the olive oil in a saucepan over a low heat. Add the garlic, chilli and parsley to the pan and stir for 30 seconds. Add the ground nuts and stir around for about one minute, being careful not to let them brown. Then stir in the remaining three tablespoons of olive oil and the hot water. Season the mixture with salt and

remove the saucepan from the heat. Add the sliced basil leaves to the pecan nut mixture.

Bring a large pan of salted water to the boil, add the spaghetti and cook until the pasta is *al dente* – cooked, but still with a slight bite to it. Then drain the pasta, put it into the warmed serving bowl and mix the pecan mixture in thoroughly.
Serves 4

▶ *Tagliatelle with rocket, orange zest and hazelnut oil; spaghetti with peas, spring onions and pea, mint and smetana sauce; spaghetti with pecan nuts, parsley, basil and red chilli*

BUTTER BEANS WITH SMOKY COURGETTE PURÉE

When using dried beans, older beans will need longer cooking.

250g (8oz) dried butter beans
2 large sprigs of fresh rosemary
8–10 fresh bay leaves
500g (1lb) ripe plum tomatoes
40g (1½oz) butter
2 teaspoons chopped fresh rosemary
2 teaspoons golden caster sugar
500g (1lb) courgettes
Olive oil, for brushing
2 tablespoons fromage frais
Salt and black pepper

Soak the beans overnight. Drain them and bring them to the boil in fresh, unsalted water with the rosemary sprigs and bay leaves. Simmer gently for 20–40 minutes until just soft right through.

Meanwhile, cover the tomatoes with boiling water for two minutes, then drain, peel, and halve them lengthways. Melt the butter in a sauté pan over a medium heat and add the tomatoes and the chopped rosemary. Stir the tomatoes gently for about five minutes. Then stir in the sugar and remove the pan from the heat. When the beans are ready, remove the herbs, drain the beans and put them in a serving bowl. Stir in the tomato mixture and season to taste. Keep warm.

Top and tail the courgettes and halve lengthways. Smear them with olive oil and sprinkle with salt on both sides, then grill them, skin side upwards, until the skin has blackened. Purée them together with the fromage frais. Season to taste and serve with the butter beans.
Serves 4

CANNELLINI BEANS WITH LEMONY DILL SAUCE

This delicate creamy sauce is lovely either with cannellini or haricot beans.

175g (6oz) dried cannellini beans
2 tablespoons olive oil
FOR THE SAUCE:
150ml (¼ pint) double cream
Finely grated zest and juice of
   1 lemon
Handful of fresh dill, chopped finely
Salt and black pepper

Soak the beans in cold water overnight. Then drain them and put them into a saucepan with plenty of unsalted water. Bring the beans to the boil and simmer for 30–50 minutes (older pulses will take longer) until they are soft but not breaking up.

Drain the beans, and put them into a warm serving bowl. Stir in the olive oil, and keep the beans in a warm place while you make the sauce.

To make the sauce, put the cream and the lemon zest into a saucepan. Bring to the boil and bubble, stirring, for two minutes. Then remove the pan from the heat and gradually stir in the lemon juice, followed by the chopped dill. Season to taste with salt and plenty of black pepper. Mix the sauce into the cooked beans and serve immediately for a light meal with bread or salad.
Serves 4

LENTIL TART WITH RICE CRUNCH PASTRY

This is reminiscent of traditional vegetarian fare and is perfect for a homely informal meal.

FOR THE PASTRY:
175g (6oz) plain flour
1 teaspoon salt
25g (1oz) ground rice
125g (4oz) butter
1 tablespoon water
FOR THE LENTIL FILLING:
1 onion, chopped finely
175g (6oz) orange lentils
600ml (1 pint) milk
1 teaspoon ground mace
3–5 pinches of chilli powder
1 large egg (size 1)
50g (2oz) grated cheese (Cheddar
   or Cheshire)
Paprika, to sprinkle
Salt

To make the pastry, sift the flour and salt into a bowl and stir in the ground rice. Put the butter and water in a saucepan and melt the butter gently. Then pour the butter into the flour mixture, stirring it in with a wooden spoon to form a warm dough. Press this dough evenly over the base and sides of a 23cm (9-inch) loose-bottomed flan tin, bringing it up slightly above the rim of the tin. Refrigerate the pastry while you make the filling.

Put the chopped onion into a saucepan with the lentils and the milk. Simmer very gently in the open pan, stirring now and then, for 45–60 minutes, until the mixture is thick and mushy. Stir in the ground mace and season to taste with salt and chilli powder. Leave until cool. Set the oven to preheat at Gas Mark 5/190°C/375°F.

Whisk the egg and stir it into the cooled lentil mixture. Spoon the mixture into the pastry case and sprinkle over the grated cheese. Lastly, sprinkle sparingly with paprika. Cook in the centre of the oven for 35–45 minutes or until the filling has set.

Remove the tart from the oven and leave it in the tin for a few minutes. Then push up the tart out of the tin sides very carefully. Using a long wide spatula, ease the tart off the base of the tin on to a flat, round serving plate.
TO SERVE Serve with fresh tomato sauce made with juicy ripe tomatoes and a mixed, crisp salad.
Serves 4–5

▶ *Butter beans with smoky courgette purée; cannellini beans with lemony dill sauce; lentil tart with rice crunch pastry*

EGG & CHEESE DISHES

During my early childhood, for no very good reason, I decided I didn't like eggs. Luckily, the first omelette I tasted on a holiday in France made me realise how silly I had been. Soon after that I picked up a new-laid egg from my grandmother's hen hutch and she poached it for me; I had to admit that I had never tasted anything quite so good as that light and creamy-textured white with the orange yolk running over it. I cannot imagine where I would be without eggs; what would life be like without the cakes, omelettes, soufflés, real vanilla ice creams, mayonnaise, sauces and all the other miracles that eggs produce in the kitchen? Eggs provide a richness of flavour and wide variation of textures. The yolks can make sauces satin-smooth while thickening them to just the right degree and the fluffy lightness of the whites make a mixture rise to astonishing heights. Cheese, equally versatile, combines naturally with eggs and enhances many other ingredients. Leafy salads are at their most irresistible when speckled with thinly shaved or grated Parmesan. Vegetables with a gratin of melted cheese on top are always welcome. In fact, cheese dishes are the most popular choice for light but nutritious meals and snacks.

CAULIFLOWER CHEESE WITH SUN-DRIED TOMATOES, FRESH RED CHILLI AND CRUNCHY PARMESAN TOPPING

I have never grown out of a fondness for good nursery food, although too often it is rather bland. Not so, however, with this more sophisticated version of an old favourite.

1 large cauliflower
1 fresh green chilli
50g (2oz) butter
2 garlic cloves, chopped finely
8–10 sun-dried tomatoes, sliced
2 tablespoons plain flour
600ml (1 pint) milk
300ml (½ pint) natural yogurt
175g (6oz) grated cheese (pecorino or Cheddar)
FOR THE TOPPING:
2 tablespoons white breadcrumbs
1 tablespoon grated Parmesan
2 tablespoons olive oil
Salt and black pepper

◄ *Cauliflower cheese with sun-dried tomatoes, fresh red chilli and crunchy Parmesan topping*

Break up the cauliflower into medium-sized florets. Either boil or steam the florets until they are just soft. Drain and arrange the cauliflower in a large, fairly shallow ovenproof dish.

Cut open the chilli lengthways under running water, discard the seeds and stem and then chop the chilli flesh finely. Melt the butter gently in a large saucepan over a medium heat. Add the garlic to the melted butter in the pan and stir around for about one minute, then remove the saucepan from the heat. Using a wooden spoon, stir in the sliced sun-dried tomatoes and the chopped chilli. Then stir in the flour until the mixture is smooth. Gradually stir in the milk, a little at a time, followed by the natural yogurt.

Return the saucepan to the heat and bring the mixture to the boil, stirring it in one direction only (this prevents the yogurt curdling) until the mixture thickens. Allow the mixture to bubble, still stirring all the time, for 2–3 minutes. Then add the grated Cheddar or pecorino cheese and stir until the cheese has melted.

Remove the saucepan from the heat. Season the sauce to taste with a little salt (the cheese adds a certain saltiness to the sauce anyway) and black pepper and then pour it over the cauliflower in the ovenproof dish.

To make the topping, put the breadcrumbs into a bowl and stir in the grated Parmesan cheese and olive oil. Mix together thoroughly and season with black pepper.

Sprinkle the topping mixture evenly over the cheese sauce and the cauliflower. Put the cauliflower cheese under a preheated grill until the top is nicely browned. If you are not quite ready to eat, you can keep this dish warm in a low oven for up to 30 minutes. Serve warm.

TO SERVE This can be served as a main dish or as an accompaniment.
Serves 4 as a main dish

THREE-CHEESE CUSTARD

This savoury baked egg custard is topped with a rich cheese and chive sauce and makes an excellent lunch or supper dish.

FOR THE CUSTARD:
    4 large eggs (size 1)
    600ml (1 pint) milk
    50g (2oz) mature Cheddar cheese, grated finely
    ½ teaspoon freshly grated nutmeg
    Salt and black pepper
FOR THE SAUCE:
    50g (2oz) butter
    25g (1oz) plain flour
    300ml (½ pint) milk
    75g (3oz) Gruyère or Emmental cheese, grated
    1 egg yolk
    3 pinches of chilli powder
    2 rounded tablespoons fresh chives, chopped
    50g (2oz) Parmesan cheese, grated

Half-fill a roasting tin with water and place it in the centre of an oven set to preheat at Gas Mark 2/150°C/300°F. While the oven is heating, make the custard. Break the eggs into a mixing bowl and whisk lightly. Heat the milk in a saucepan to just below boiling point and stir in the Cheddar cheese until melted. Remove the pan from the heat and whisk the hot milk into the eggs, a little at a time. Whisk in the grated nutmeg and season well with salt and black pepper. Pour the custard mixture into a buttered round 1.2-litre (2-pint) ovenproof dish. Place the dish in the roasting tin of water and bake for 1¼ to 1½ hours, or until the custard feels firm to a light touch in the centre. If the custard begins to brown during cooking, cover it loosely with foil.

While the custard is cooking, make the sauce. Melt the butter in a saucepan over a low heat, remove the pan from the heat and stir in the flour using a wooden spoon. Gradually stir in the milk, then place the saucepan back on the heat and bring the mixture to the boil, stirring all the time. Reduce the heat and simmer for 2–3 minutes, stirring constantly.

Remove the sauce from the heat and stir in the Gruyère or Emmental cheese. When the cheese has melted, stir in the egg yolk thoroughly, then season with the chilli powder and salt to taste and stir in the chopped chives. Finally, pour the sauce gradually over the custard and sprinkle generously with the Parmesan cheese. Place the custard under a medium grill until the top is golden brown in patches, and serve immediately.
TO SERVE Serve accompanied by a green salad and warm crusty bread or Tomato, Herb, Parmesan & Garlic Bread (see page 151).
Serves 4

CHEESE, SPINACH AND SORREL ROULADE

If you can't get sorrel for this pretty roulade, try substituting rocket or a mixture of spinach and watercress.

    2 tablespoons Parmesan, grated
    375g (12oz) fresh spinach, chopped finely
    Handful of sorrel leaves
    50g (2oz) fresh white breadcrumbs
    175g (6oz) mature Cheddar cheese, grated finely
    4 large eggs (size 1), separated
    150ml (¼ pint) single cream
    3 rounded tablespoons 8% fat fromage frais
    3 teaspoons bottled green peppercorns
    Salt
    3–4 pinches of chilli powder
    Mixed salad leaves and herbs, to garnish

Set the oven to preheat at Gas Mark 6/200°C/400°F. Line a 23 x 33cm (9 x 13-inch) Swiss roll tin with a piece of buttered baking parchment and sprinkle it evenly with a thin layer of grated Parmesan. Place the chopped spinach in a saucepan with very little salted water, cover and cook for 3–5 minutes or until the spinach is soft. Drain the spinach, pressing between double layers of kitchen paper to dry thoroughly; then leave it on one side. Slice the sorrel into very thin strips and leave it separately on one side.

Mix the breadcrumbs and grated Cheddar cheese together in a mixing bowl. Using a wooden spoon, stir in the egg yolks, cream and the sliced sorrel leaves. Season the mixture with salt and chilli powder to taste. Place the egg whites in a separate bowl, add a pinch of salt and whisk until they stand in soft peaks; then, using a metal spoon, fold them gently into the cheese mixture. Pour the cheese and egg mixture into the tin and bake in the centre of the oven for 10–15 minutes or until the roulade has risen and is firm to a light touch in the middle. Remove the roulade from the oven and leave to cool in the tin — it will shrink slightly. Sprinkle a little cold water over a clean tea towel to dampen it, lay the towel on top of the roulade and leave until completely cold.

Meanwhile, spoon the fromage frais into a bowl and stir in the cooked spinach. Crush the green peppercorns roughly with a pestle and mortar and add them to the mixture together with a little salt to taste. When the roulade is cold, sprinkle a sheet of baking parchment slightly larger than the roulade all over with grated Parmesan. Remove the tea towel from the roulade, loosen the edges with a knife and turn the roulade out on to the baking parchment. Spread the roulade evenly with the spinach mixture and then roll it up fairly loosely with the help of the baking parchment to form a Swiss roll.
TO SERVE Cut the roulade into eight slices with a sharp knife and serve them on individual plates. Garnish each slice with a few salad leaves.
Serves 8

▶ *Three-cheese custard; cheese, spinach and sorrel roulade*

DEEP-FRIED FETA CHEESE AND MUSHROOMS
IN BEER AND CARAWAY BATTER

You can use this lovely batter for frying all sorts of raw vegetables to make light crisp fritters, which can then be served either as a first course or as an accompaniment to a main dish. The beer makes the batter lighter and crispier.

125g (4oz) self-raising flour
1 teaspoon salt
½ teaspoon chilli powder
2 teaspoons caraway seeds
1 egg (size 3)
150ml (¼ pint) beer
250g (8oz) feta cheese
Flour, for coating
250g (8oz) chestnut mushrooms
Oil for deep frying

Sift the flour, salt and chilli powder into a food processor. Then add the caraway seeds and the egg. Whizz the mixture briefly together; then gradually add the beer, whizzing between each addition. Pour the batter into a large bowl and leave it to one side for at least 20 minutes.

Meanwhile, cut the feta cheese into 2.5cm (1-inch) cubes and roll each cube in flour to coat it. Slice the mushrooms in half lengthways unless they are very small.

Heat a large pan of oil suitable for deep frying over a high heat until the oil is smoking – groundnut oil is a good choice. Put the prepared feta cheese and mushrooms into the bowl of batter and stir the pieces around to coat them thoroughly. Spoon up separate batter-coated pieces of feta or mushroom and put them into the hot oil in batches. Deep-fry the pieces until the batter is golden and crisp. Remove the pieces carefully with a slotted spoon and place them on sheets of kitchen paper to drain.

TO SERVE . As soon as all the pieces are cooked, pile them up on a bed of leaves arranged on a pretty serving dish or on four individual plates. Serve the fritters immediately while they are still warm.

Serves 4

PUFFED RICOTTA AND GORGONZOLA ROLL
WITH SUN-DRIED TOMATOES

This delicious crispy and soft roll, with a mixture of Italian cheeses, is easy to make and excellent for a light lunch or supper. If you prefer, you can prepare it several hours in advance, keep it in the refrigerator and then simply pop it in the oven to cook it fresh. If you can get the sun-dried tomatoes sold in jars of oil, they are nice and soft, and their flavour is wonderful with rich, strong cheeses, such as Gorgonzola. As an alternative, you can use grated mature pecorino or any other strongly-flavoured Italian cheese.

250g (8oz) puff pastry
250g (8oz) ricotta cheese
175g (6oz) Gorgonzola cheese or
   strongly-flavoured Italian cheese
8 sun-dried tomatoes
   (approximately), sliced thinly
10 fresh basil or sage leaves
   (approximately), sliced in strips
1 egg
1 egg yolk
Salt and black pepper
Grated Parmesan, to sprinkle
Basil or sage leaves, to garnish

Roll the pastry out on a flat surface into a rectangle about 20 x 25cm (8 x 10 inches). Prick the pastry all over with a fork. Put the ricotta cheese into a bowl and crumble in the Gorgonzola. Add the sliced sun-dried tomatoes and the sage or basil leaves. Whisk the egg lightly in a cup and add to the cheese in the bowl. Season the cheese mixture with a little salt and plenty of black pepper and mix together with a wooden spoon.

Spread the mixture on to the pastry within 1cm (½ inch) of the edges. Moisten the edges and then roll the pastry up loosely. Press the ends lightly together to seal in the filling. Transfer the pastry carefully to a greased baking sheet. If you are not ready to cook the pastry roll at once, refrigerate it until needed.

When you are ready, preheat the oven to Gas Mark 7/220°C/425°F. Brush the roll all over with the egg yolk; then make slanting slashes with a sharp knife along the top at 2.5cm (1-inch) intervals. Sprinkle the roll lightly with the grated Parmesan cheese.

Sprinkle the baking sheet with a little water all around the roll (but do not dampen the roll itself). Cook on a high shelf of the oven, for 20–30 minutes, or until the pastry has risen and is a rich golden brown. Garnish with basil or sage leaves.

Serves 4

▲ *Puffed ricotta and Gorgonzola roll with sun-dried tomatoes*

◄ *Deep-fried feta cheese and mushrooms in beer and caraway batter*

DEVONIAN SPANISH OMELETTE

Every summer, we have a picnic beside the River Dart in Devon, and we always have this thick Spanish omelette, packed with good things. Served either warm or cold, it is always delicious.

1 large red pepper
1 large yellow pepper
375g (12oz) onions
2 small garlic cloves
2 tablespoons olive oil
25g (1oz) butter
300g (10oz) firm-textured potatoes, boiled and cubed
10 sun-dried tomatoes, sliced thinly
10 large eggs (size 1)
75g (3oz) coarsely grated cheese or 50g (2oz) grated Parmesan cheese
2 handfuls of fresh mixed herbs, including dill, chopped roughly
Salt and black pepper

Cut open the red and yellow peppers lengthways and remove the seeds and stem. Slice the onions finely. Chop the garlic finely. Put the olive oil and butter into a large, deep, heavy-based frying pan – about 25cm (10 inches) in diameter – over a fairly low heat. Add the garlic to the pan and cook gently for one minute. Add the sliced onions and continue to cook gently, stirring around occasionally. Meanwhile, put the peppers, skin side upwards, under a very hot grill until the skin has blackened. Remove the peppers, and put them into a paper bag until they are cool enough to handle. Then peel off the skin and slice thinly.

When the onions are really soft but not browned, add the cubed potatoes, the sliced peppers and the sliced sun-dried tomatoes. Stir to mix and remove from the heat. Break the eggs into a bowl and whisk together lightly. Stir in the grated cheese and chopped herbs and a good seasoning of salt and black pepper. Pour this mixture into the frying pan of ingredients, stir once and return the pan to a low heat. Cook for about 15 minutes until all but the central part is set; then cover the pan with foil and continue cooking for a few more minutes until the omelette is set to a light touch in the centre. If you want, you can put the frying pan under a grill to brown the top.

TO SERVE Cut the omelette like a cake straight from the pan. If you are taking this on a picnic, take it along still in the pan you cooked it in, wrapped in greaseproof paper and layers of newspaper to keep it hot.
Serves 6–8

EGG, CHEESE AND ONION GRATIN WITH CHERRY TOMATOES

Cheese dishes are always popular with children and adults alike, and this is one of those soothing, family supper dishes which everybody will welcome after a tiring day. Sage and cheese together are particularly good, and the whole cherry tomatoes add a fresh juiciness. It could be accompanied by any number of things, but you can serve it with a green vegetable, such as steamed broccoli, or with a salad, and waxy-textured new potatoes are also very good.

8 large eggs (size 1–2)
250g (8oz) cherry tomatoes
10 fresh sage leaves (approximately), chopped
65g (2½oz) butter
¼ whole nutmeg, grated
50g (2oz) plain flour
450ml (¾ pint) milk
125g (4oz) strong-flavoured grated cheese
2 large onions
Salt
4–5 pinches of chilli powder
Chives, to garnish

◄ *Devonian Spanish omelette*

Semi-hard boil the eggs (7–8 minutes from the time you lower them into the boiling water). Cool in a sink of cold water; then peel and cut them across in thick slices. Put the egg slices on the bottom of a fairly shallow ovenproof dish. Arrange the cherry tomatoes among the slices of egg. Scatter the chopped sage over the top.

Set the oven to preheat at Gas Mark 6/200°C/400°F. Melt 50g (2oz) of the butter in a heavy-based saucepan over a medium heat. Remove the pan from the heat and stir in the nutmeg. Then stir in the flour until the mixture is smooth. Gradually add the milk, stirring all the time. Put the pan back over the heat and bring the mixture to the boil. Bubble gently, still stirring, for 2–3 minutes until the sauce is thick and smooth. Then add the grated cheese and stir until melted. Remove the pan from the heat and season to taste with salt and the chilli powder.

Slice the onions across thinly in rings. Melt the remaining butter in a heavy-based frying pan and fry the onion rings over a fairly high heat until soft and golden brown. Then stir the onions into the cheese sauce mixture. Spoon the sauce over the eggs and tomatoes in the dish. Put the dish near the top of the preheated oven, and bake for 20–30 minutes or until the top of the gratin has turned a rich golden brown. Serve garnished with chives.
Serves 4–5

▲ *Egg, cheese and onion gratin with cherry tomatoes*

Oven-baked Pancake Rolled with Goats' Cheese, Tomatoes and Basil

The taste of melting hot goats' cheese is, for me, one of the really supreme gastronomic pleasures. One day, I developed this dish entirely for my own satisfaction. Yellow tomatoes look especially pretty in the filling.

FOR THE PANCAKE BATTER:
4 tablespoons olive oil
40g (1½oz) plain flour
1 large egg (size 1)
150ml (¼ pint) milk
FOR THE FILLING:
1 egg
325g (11oz) soft fresh goats' cheese
8–10 basil leaves, sliced thinly
75g (3oz) yellow or red cherry
*   tomatoes*
2 tablespoons olive oil
Grated Parmesan cheese, to sprinkle
Salt and black pepper

To make the batter, preheat the oven to Gas Mark 9/240°C/475°F, then simply put all the ingredients in a food processor with a generous pinch of salt and whizz thoroughly until the mixture is completely smooth. Generously butter a 23 x 33cm (9 x 13-inch) roasting tin. Put the tin on the top shelf of the preheated oven for a few minutes to heat up. Then pour the batter into the hot tin, put the tin back in the oven and cook for 10 minutes or until the batter is risen and golden. Remove the tin from the oven. Turn the cooked batter out on to a flat surface and cover it with a clean and slightly damp cloth. Turn down the oven to Gas Mark 4/180°C/350°F.

For the filling, put the egg into a bowl and whisk lightly. Then add the soft goats' cheese and mix thoroughly together with a wooden spoon. Add the sliced basil leaves to the egg and cheese mixture. Season with salt and plenty of freshly ground black pepper. Lastly, halve the cherry tomatoes and fold them into the cheese mixture.

Remove the cloth from the pancake. Spread the filling mixture evenly all over the pancake and then roll it up loosely, from the short end, like a Swiss roll. Oil a shallow, rectangular ovenproof dish and lay the roll carefully in it, join side down. Smear the top with olive oil and sprinkle generously with grated Parmesan.

Cook the pancake in the centre of a preheated oven, , for 20–25 minutes.
TO SERVE Serve immediately, accompanied by a green salad with a sharp vinaigrette dressing.
Serves 4

Soft Goats' Cheese Soufflés on a Fresh Tomato Base

These individual soufflés make a practical hot first course as they can be prepared in advance, up to the point before you fold in the whisked egg whites, and then freshly cooked minutes before serving. Cooked goats' cheese is always delicious, especially here with a hint of oregano and juicy tomatoes underneath.

6 ripe tomatoes
2 teaspoons caster sugar
150g (5oz) fresh soft goats' cheese
1 teaspoon cornflour
3 large eggs (size 1)
½ teaspoon dried oregano
Grated Parmesan cheese, to sprinkle
Salt and black pepper

Butter six deep cocotte dishes, spreading the butter generously on the bottom and more thinly up the sides. Put the tomatoes in a bowl, pour boiling water over to cover them, and leave them for 1–2 minutes. Drain, skin and chop the tomatoes very finely and put the pieces back into the bowl,

including any juices. Stir in the caster sugar and a good seasoning of salt and black pepper. Divide the tomato mixture evenly between the six buttered dishes.

Put the soft goats' cheese into a bowl. Add the cornflour and mix it in thoroughly with a wooden spoon. Separate two of the eggs (putting the egg whites into a large bowl) and mix the egg yolks into the cheese mixture until the mixture is very smooth. Stir in the oregano and season well with salt and freshly ground black pepper.

Just before you are ready to eat, set the oven to preheat at Gas Mark 6/200°C/400°F. Put the prepared cocotte dishes together on a baking sheet. Separate the remaining egg and add the egg white to the reserved egg white (the yolk can be used in another dish). Add half a teaspoon of salt to the egg whites and whisk until they stand in soft peaks. Then, using a metal spoon, fold them gently into the cheese mixture. Spoon the cheese mixture into the buttered dishes on top of the tomato base and sprinkle the surface lightly with grated Parmesan cheese. Bake in

the centre of the oven for 10–12 minutes or until they are well risen and nicely browned. Serve at once.
Serves 6

▲ *Soft goats' cheese soufflés on a fresh tomato base*

◄ *Oven-baked pancake rolled with goats' cheese, tomatoes and basil*

BILLOWED EGGS BAKED ON RADICCHIO

This is a different way of preparing eggs; the whisked whites set in a soft froth around the yolks.

> 3 tablespoons olive oil
> 375–500g (12oz–1lb) radicchio, sliced roughly
> 4 large eggs (size 1)
> *FOR THE SAUCE:*
> 25g (1oz) butter
> 15g (½oz) plain flour, sifted
> 300ml (½ pint) milk
> 2 teaspoons dried oregano
> 65g (2½oz) grated Cheddar cheese
> 4 rounded teaspoons coarse grain mustard
> Chilli powder
> Salt

Put the olive oil into a large, deep frying pan over a medium heat. Add the sliced radicchio and stir for a few minutes until the leaves are just soft. Spread them on the bottom of a lightly buttered, shallow ovenproof dish and keep on one side. Set the oven to preheat at Gas Mark 7/220°C/425°F.

To make the sauce, melt the butter in the saucepan, remove the pan from the heat and stir in the sifted flour until smooth. Gradually stir in the milk and add the oregano. Return the pan to the heat and bring the sauce to the boil, stirring all the time. Simmer, still stirring, for about three minutes. Then add the grated cheese and the mustard and stir until the cheese has melted.

Lastly, add salt and chilli powder to taste. Remove the pan from the heat, cover and leave it in a warm place.

Carefully separate the eggs, putting the whole yolks in one bowl and putting the whites into a separate bowl. Add a pinch of salt to the egg whites and whisk until they stand in soft peaks. Spoon the whites into the dish all over the radicchio. Make four holes in the whisked egg white and gently slide a yolk into each. Bake just above the centre of the oven for 7–10 minutes, or until the yolks are just softly set. Serve at once, pouring the cheese sauce around the eggs.
TO SERVE Serve with toast and salad.
Serves 4

HARD-BOILED EGGS IN CURRIED SAUCE

Here is a recipe which tastes delicious and homemade, but is so easy and quick to make it seems like cheating.

> 8 large eggs (size 1)
> Large handful of fresh coriander leaves
> 175g (6oz) fromage frais
> 2–3 teaspoons mild curry paste
> 2 tablespoons Greek yogurt
> Salt

Semi-hard boil the eggs for eight minutes from the time the water returns to the boil after adding the eggs. Drain the eggs and put them into a sink of cold water to cool slightly before peeling and slicing in half. Arrange the halves in a warmed, shallow serving dish. Remove eight small sprigs of coriander and chop up the remainder as finely as possible. Put the fromage frais into a saucepan over a fairly low heat,

and, using a wooden spoon, stir in two teaspoons of the curry paste. Then stir in the yogurt until the mixture is smooth. Finally stir in the finely chopped coriander and season the sauce with salt to taste. Add another teaspoonful of curry paste if you think the sauce needs it. Spoon the sauce over the egg halves and garnish with the reserved coriander.
Serves 6

EGGS POACHED ON A BED OF ONIONS AND CHICORY

Onions are sweet, and chicory has a subtle bitterness, and this combined with a mild bite of chilli tastes excellent in this simple dish. Serve with good crusty bread to mop up the delicious juices.

> 3 large chicory
> 1 fresh red or green chilli
> 50g (2oz) butter
> 150ml (¼ pint) vegetable stock
> 4 onions, sliced in thin rings
> 2 teaspoons caster sugar
> Generous handful of flat leaf parsley, chopped roughly
> 4 large eggs (size 1)
> Salt
> Chilli powder

Cut off the base of the chicory and cut it across in 1cm (½-inch) pieces. Cut the chilli open under running water, discard the seeds and stem and then slice the flesh across thinly. Melt the butter in a large, deep frying pan over a medium heat and then pour in the stock. Add the onions for 4–5 minutes. Then add the chicory and the chilli to the pan. Allow the mixture to bubble gently over a low heat, stirring occasionally, until the vegetables are really soft. If all the liquid is not evaporated, increase the heat and continue to bubble until there is no liquid left. Then stir in the sugar and cook for one minute. Remove the pan

from the heat. Season the mixture to taste with salt and chilli powder. Stir the chopped parsley into the onion and chicory mixture. Then level the mixture and, using a spoon, make four hollows in it. Carefully break an egg into each hollow.

Now cover the frying pan with a lid or a piece of foil and put it back over a fairly low heat for 3–5 minutes or until the whites of the eggs have set — don't allow the egg yolks to become at all hard. Serve straight from the pan.

▶ *Billowed eggs baked on radicchio; hard-boiled eggs in curried sauce; eggs poached on a bed of onions and chicory*

VEGETABLE SIDE DISHES

This chapter is far removed from the accompanying vegetable dishes which you might have had in many British or American homes 30 years ago. We have come to appreciate vegetables far more in recent years, a much greater variety are available and we have learned to cook them properly. We have also realized from foreign travel and cuisines that instead of serving, for example, separate bowls of unseasoned greens and plain boiled potatoes simply as accompaniments to the main dish, vegetables can be combined both with each other and with herbs, spices, interesting oils or other aromatic seasonings to become a much more important part of the meal. Three or four contrasting dishes taken from this chapter, served together, would make a satisfying vegetarian meal, or they can be served with a main course of chicken or fish. Mixing vegetables together when they have been cooked in different ways can produce an exciting combination of textures and often looks decorative too. The fact that vegetables are so varied in taste, form and texture, and that they contain flavours ranging from stimulatingly bitter to softly sweet has made this one of the most pleasurable chapters to work on. It has left me feeling that I want to try out all sorts of other combinations.

SAUTÉED MUSHROOMS AND BROCCOLI
WITH GARLIC AND CORIANDER SEEDS

This simple but delicious mixture is very lightly and quickly cooked so that the broccoli remains slightly crunchy. It can be served either as one of several vegetable dishes to make up a varied vegetarian meal, or as an accompaniment to grilled chicken or fish.

250g (8oz) broccoli
4 tablespoons olive oil
2 large garlic cloves
1 teaspoon coriander seeds
250g (8oz) chestnut or other firm
  mushrooms
Salt
Black pepper

◄ *Sautéed mushrooms and broccoli with garlic and coriander seeds.*

Cut any thick stalks off the broccoli and peel and cut them into fairly thin pieces. Divide the broccoli spears into medium-sized florets. Steam or boil both the florets and the sliced stalks until they are just soft but still retain their bright green colour. As soon as the broccoli is cooked, submerge it in cold water to stop the cooking process, then drain the broccoli through a strainer when cold.

Put the olive oil in a sauté pan over a medium heat. Chop the cloves of garlic as finely as possible. Grind the coriander seeds in a pestle and mortar (or, alternatively, place them in a small plastic bag, such as a freezer bag, or in an envelope, and crush them with a rolling pin or mallet). Using a sharp knife, slice the mushrooms into 5mm (¼-inch) slices. Add the crushed coriander seeds and the sliced mushrooms to the oil in the sauté pan and stir around until the mushrooms are just soft.

Then add the two finely chopped cloves of garlic and stir for one minute. Lastly, add the drained broccoli to the pan and stir for a further 30 seconds. Remove the sauté pan from the heat and season the broccoli and mushroom mixture with salt and plenty of black pepper.

TO SERVE Turn into a heated serving bowl. You can also serve this dish at room temperature, which is just as good as it is served hot.

Serves 4

PARSNIPS WITH SHIITAKE MUSHROOMS IN MUSTARD SAUCE

This makes a good side dish or main course, with a green vegetable or salad.

750g (1½lb) parsnips
Seasoned flour, for coating
6 tablespoons olive oil
6 shiitake mushrooms
FOR THE SAUCE:
25g (1oz) butter
1 tablespoon cornflour
300ml (½ pint) milk
1 teaspoon white wine vinegar
2 teaspoons coarse grain mustard
2 tablespoons natural yogurt
Generous handful of parsley, chopped finely
Salt and black pepper

Top and tail the parsnips and slice them across into 5mm (¼-inch) rounds. Steam or boil them until they are just tender. Pat the parsnips dry with kitchen paper and then dip them into a little seasoned flour. Put the olive oil into a large frying pan over a medium heat and sauté the parsnips until the slices are golden brown all over, adding a little more olive oil if necessary. Using a slotted spatula, transfer the parsnips to a wide, shallow serving dish, reserving the oil in the pan. Keep the parsnip slices warm in a very low oven.

Thinly slice the shiitake mushrooms. Add them to the reserved oil in the frying pan, and stir around for 3–4 minutes, or until they are just soft. Add the mushrooms to the parsnip slices in the oven.

Finally, to make the sauce, melt the butter in a saucepan over a moderate heat and stir in the cornflour until smooth. Slowly stir in the milk, bring the mixture to the boil and allow it to bubble for about three minutes, stirring all the time. Add the vinegar, mustard and the yogurt and season to taste.

Lastly, stir in the chopped fresh parsley and pour the sauce unevenly over the parsnip mixture in the serving dish just before taking it to the table.
Serves 4 as a side dish

SLICED BRUSSELS SPROUTS WITH GARLIC AND CARAWAY SEEDS

One can get very bored with whole, boiled brussels sprouts but they do taste good. Here the sprouts are thinly sliced and cooked in butter and a little water.

750–875g (1½–1¾lb) brussels sprouts
75g (3oz) unsalted butter
150ml (¼ pint) water
2 garlic cloves, chopped finely
½ teaspoon caraway seeds
Salt and black pepper

Cut off the bases of the sprouts and remove any loose or damaged outer leaves. Then slice the sprouts across thinly lengthways. Put the unsalted butter and water into a saucepan over a medium heat. When the butter has melted and the mixture is bubbling, add the sprouts. Cover the pan and simmer for 3–4 minutes or until the sprouts are bright green and soft when pierced with a fork. Then remove the pan lid and add the chopped garlic and caraway seeds. Stir the sprouts around in the open pan for 1–2 minutes or until all the water has evaporated.

Lastly, season with salt and black pepper and spoon the sprout mixture on to a serving dish.
TO SERVE This dish goes particularly well with plainly roasted poultry or game birds.
Serves 6

BRAISED RED CABBAGE WITH CHESTNUTS AND PETITS POIS

This dish is a perfect accompaniment to game birds, but it can also be served on its own as a light meal.

875g–1kg (1¾–2lb) red cabbage
300ml (½ pint) chicken or vegetable stock
50g (2oz) butter
4 tablespoons sherry vinegar
2 teaspoons dill seeds
3 teaspoons dried green peppercorns
2 rounded tablespoons redcurrant jelly
500g (1lb) frozen petits pois
425g (14oz) vacuum-packed chestnuts
Salt and black pepper

Cut the red cabbage in half, remove the core, and slice into smallish pieces. Put the stock, butter and vinegar into a casserole or heavy-based saucepan and place the pan over a medium heat.

When the butter has melted, add the dill seeds, the peppercorns and the sliced cabbage. Stir to mix thoroughly; then bring the liquid up to boiling point, cover the dish and lower the heat to simmer very gently for 30–40 minutes or until the red cabbage is really soft and mushy.

Add the redcurrant jelly to the cabbage and stir until the jelly has melted. Then add the frozen petits pois. Bring the cabbage to the boil again and bubble fiercely in the open pan for a few minutes until the juices have almost evaporated. Finally, season the cabbage to taste with salt and pepper and gently stir in the whole chestnuts. Cover the pan and leave it over a low heat for a few minutes before serving so that the chestnuts warm through.
TO SERVE If there are no accompanying dishes, I add more chestnuts to this, or sometimes chickpeas instead. Then all it needs is some warm crusty bread.
Serves 6–8

▶ *Parsnips with shiitake mushrooms in mustard sauce; sliced brussels sprouts with garlic and caraway seeds; braised red cabbage with chestnuts and petits pois*

HERBED SWEET POTATO AND ONION GRATINÉE

Check the colour of the potato flesh by scraping away a little skin; they all have the same chestnut-like flavour, but the orange-fleshed ones are far prettier.

4 tablespoons olive oil
3 large onions, chopped finely
3 large garlic cloves, chopped finely
250g (8oz) sweet potatoes
2 generous sprigs of rosemary,
  chopped finely
10 fresh sage leaves
  (approximately), chopped finely
Handful of parsley, chopped finely
Salt and black pepper

Set the oven to preheat at Gas Mark 4/180°C/350°F. Put the olive oil into a large sauté pan over a medium heat. Add the onion and stir until soft and browned. Then add the garlic and stir for another 2–3 minutes. Remove the sauté pan from the heat and turn the onion mixture into a large bowl.

Peel the sweet potatoes and cut them into large pieces. Put the pieces through the grating blade of a food processor. Turn the grated potato into the bowl with the onion mixture.

Add the chopped rosemary and sage to the bowl and, using a wooden spoon,

mix all the ingredients together thoroughly. Season the mixture generously with salt and black pepper. Then spread the mixture evenly into a shallow round or rectangular ovenproof dish. Dribble a little olive oil all over the top of the sweet potato mixture and cook just above the centre of a preheated oven, for about one hour or until the dish is golden brown and crispy on top.

TO SERVE Sprinkle the chopped parsley over the top of the gratinée and serve immediately.
Serves 6

TUSCAN BROAD BEANS

It's useful to have store cupboard ideas and this is delicious, easy and quick.

575g (19oz) can of chopped
  tomatoes
50g (2oz) butter
2–3 large garlic cloves, chopped
500g (1lb) frozen broad beans
Black pepper

Put the tomatoes in a heavy saucepan and add the butter and garlic. Season generously with black pepper. Bring the mixture to the boil and add the broad beans. Bring the mixture to the boil again, then simmer in the open pan for 15–20 minutes or until the sauce has reduced and thickened and the liquid has evaporated.

TO SERVE Serve as an accompaniment to a piece of strongly-flavoured grilled fish, such as swordfish or tuna, or perhaps with simply roasted chicken or duck. If you prefer, and you have the fresh ingredients, this can be made with fresh broad beans and skinned fresh plum tomatoes.
Serves 5–6

BAKED SANDWICHED AUBERGINES

These soft baked aubergines are split and sandwiched with a paste of almonds, mint, garlic and black olives. They go well with simple chicken or vegetable dishes.

50g (2oz) blanched almonds
2 large garlic cloves, sliced
Generous handful of fresh mint leaves
3 tablespoons black olive paste
1 tablespoon tomato purée
1 egg white
4 small aubergines
2 tablespoons olive oil
Salt and black pepper
Sprigs of flat leaf parsley, to garnish

◀ *Herbed sweet potato and onion gratinée;*
Tuscan broad beans; baked sandwiched
aubergines

Set the oven to preheat at Gas Mark 4/180°C/350°F. Put a dry frying pan over a fairly high heat. Add the whole almonds and stir them around for one or two minutes, just until they start to turn brown. Reserve a few whole almonds and put the remainder into the bowl of a food processor. Whizz the almonds until they are very finely chopped. Add the garlic to the nuts together with the mint leaves and whizz thoroughly until the mixture is as smooth as possible. Add the olive paste, the tomato purée and the egg white. Season the mixture with salt and plenty of black pepper and whizz again until smooth.

Cut the aubergines in half lengthways and smear the skin with a little olive oil. Spread the cut sides of

the aubergines with the almond, mint and olive mixture and sandwich the halves back together again. Arrange them in a shallow ovenproof dish, fitting them closely together so that they can't fall apart. Add the reserved whole almonds randomly. Dribble a little more olive oil over the aubergines and then cover the dish with foil.

Place the covered dish on the centre shelf of the preheated oven for 45–60 minutes, removing the foil for the last 20 minutes of cooking time. When the aubergines are fully cooked, they should feel very soft when you stick a small sharp knife through them.

TO SERVE Before serving, garnish the aubergines with sprigs of flat leaf parsley. Serve hot.
Serves 4

DRIED BROAD BEAN PURÉE WITH GREEN VEGETABLES

This is a well-known dish from the southern Italian region of Apulia. Here food epitomizes the 'Mediterranean' diet, concentrating mainly on vegetables, grains, olive oil and fish. Although it is so simple, this is a star dish. In Italy they use one of their many different varieties of chicory as the vegetable to go with this purée — long dark green stems with leaves looking like a smaller rocket. If you cannot find the dried broad beans, you can use dried butter beans, but then you should rub the cooked beans through a strainer to remove their tougher skins before you make the purée.

250g (8oz) dried, skinned broad
beans
175g (6oz) potatoes, peeled
375g (12oz) spring greens
2 chicory
5 tablespoons extra virgin olive oil
(approximately)
Sea salt and black pepper

Cover the broad beans with cold water in a bowl, and soak them for one hour or more. Drain the beans in a strainer and put them into a casserole or heavy saucepan. Cut the peeled potatoes into fairly thick slices and lay them evenly on top of the beans. Pour in enough cold water to come about 5cm (2 inches) above the level of the potatoes. Don't add any salt at this stage. Bring the water to the boil, remove any scum with a large spoon, then cover the pan and simmer the potatoes gently for two hours. Check the beans once or twice and add a little more boiling water if necessary. By the end of cooking, the water should be almost totally absorbed.

While the beans are cooking, prepare the vegetables. Slice the spring green leaves across fairly thinly. Cut the base off the chicory and slice lengthways in quarters or in thirds, depending on the size of your chicory. When the beans are ready, beat the

beans and potatoes together vigorously with a fork to turn it to a purée, beating in the extra virgin olive oil as you do so. Season the mixture to taste with salt and pepper and then turn the mixture into a wide, warmed, serving dish. Cover the dish loosely with foil and place it in a very low oven to keep warm while you cook the vegetables.

To cook the vegetables, bring a large pan of salted water to the boil, add the sliced spring greens and chicory and boil them for about 15 minutes, or until both the greens and the chicory are soft. Drain the vegetables and put them on top of the bean purée towards the middle. Sprinkle the dish with sea salt and pepper and dribble some more extra virgin olive oil all over.
TO SERVE The purée can either be served on its own as a light meal or as an accompanying vegetable to a dish of simply prepared chicken or fish.
Serves 4 as a side dish

NEW POTATOES WITH ANCHOVY AND CHIVE CREAM

The combination of potatoes and anchovies has long been appreciated, but in this creamy, appetizing sauce I feel it has rarely been better. The anchovies give a particular tang to the sauce which, oddly, is not at all fishy. It goes well with almost anything. Use Jersey potatoes or any potato with a good smooth waxy texture. It can be served hot or cold.

750g (1½lb) new potatoes
50g (2oz) can of anchovy fillets in
olive oil
150ml (¼ pint) double cream
2 tablespoons natural yogurt
Generous bunch of fresh chives,
chopped finely
Black pepper

◀ *Dried broad bean purée with green*
vegetables

Wash the potatoes and scrub off as much of the skin as you can but do not peel them. Cut any larger potatoes in half. Either steam or boil the potatoes until they are cooked and transfer them to a mixing bowl.

Meanwhile, empty the anchovy fillets and their oil into the top of a double boiler or into a bowl set over a saucepan of simmering water. Stir constantly until the anchovies melt down into a smooth mixture. Put the cream into a saucepan, bring it to the boil and bubble the cream for 3–4 minutes until it thickens slightly, stirring all the time. Remove the cream from the heat and stir in the smooth anchovy mixture. Leave to cool. Then stir in the yogurt and season to taste with black pepper – salt shouldn't be necessary because of the salty anchovies. Lastly, stir the chopped chives into the creamy mixture. Then

pour the creamy mixture onto the potatoes. Mix them well.
Serves 6

▲ *New potatoes with anchovy and chive*
cream

RED PEPPER, BABY CARROTS AND COURGETTES COOKED IN OLIVE OIL

This is simply a delicious and very pretty and colourful combination of vegetables and different textures. If available, buy the tiny red peppers which look like fresh chillies, and get the smallest, youngest spinach leaves you can find.

250g (8oz) small spinach leaves,
  trimmed
500g (1lb) small red peppers or
  2 large red peppers
375g (12oz) baby carrots
500g (1lb) small courgettes
150ml (¼ pint) olive oil
Sea salt and black pepper

Wash and dry the spinach leaves and lay them in a large shallow serving dish, breaking up any slightly larger leaves. If you are using the tiny peppers, simply cut off the stem ends. Otherwise, cut the peppers in half lengthways, remove the seeds and stem and slice the flesh crossways in 1cm (½-inch) pieces. Cut off the ends of the carrots and slice any larger ones in half lengthways. Top and tail the courgettes, cut in half across and then slice each half downwards in thin slices.

Put the olive oil into a wide casserole over a fairly gently heat.

Add the peppers and carrots and season with sea salt and plenty of black pepper. Cover the casserole and cook gently for 20–30 minutes or until the peppers are very soft and the carrots are tender. Then stir in the sliced courgettes, cover the casserole and cook for 8–10 minutes until the courgettes are soft but still bright green. Just before serving, empty the casserole ingredients and all the olive oil and juices on to the bed of spinach leaves.
TO SERVE This goes well with any piece of poultry or fish.
Serves 6

SAUTÉED LEEKS WITH PUMPKIN SEEDS AND STEAMED SUGAR SNAP PEAS

I much prefer sugar snap peas to mange tout, but either can be used.

175–250g (6–8oz) sugar snap peas
25g (1oz) butter
3 tablespoons olive oil
500g (1lb) leeks, thinly sliced in
  rings
25g (1oz) pumpkin seeds
Salt and black pepper

Pinch off the ends of the peas and put the peas on one side.

Melt the butter with the olive oil in a deep sauté pan over a medium heat. Add the prepared leeks and the pumpkin seeds and stir often until the leeks are soft but not browned. Season with salt and plenty of black pepper. Meanwhile, bring a saucepan of salted water to the boil, add the prepared peas

and boil for a few minutes until they are just soft and still bright green. Drain the peas and mix them in with the leeks. Turn the mixture into a heated serving dish.
TO SERVE Like the dish above, this simple combination could be served as a vegetable side dish or as part of a varied vegetarian meal.
Serves 4

SAUTÉED JERUSALEM ARTICHOKES WITH CHINESE LEAF

The subtle flavour of jerusalem artichokes is brought out in this dish.

500g (1lb) jerusalem artichokes
½ Chinese leaf (root end)
1 fresh red chilli
2 handfuls of flat leaf parsley
50g (2oz) butter
2 tablespoons sunflower oil
1 tablespoon sesame oil
2 large garlic cloves, chopped finely
Soy sauce, to sprinkle
Salt and black pepper

◀ *Red pepper, baby carrots and courgettes cooked in olive oil; sautéed leeks with pumpkin seeds and steamed sugar snap peas; sautéed jerusalem artichokes with Chinese leaf*

If you are unable to get jerusalem artichokes, small turnips can be used very successfully, and if you cannot get Chinese leaf, savoy cabbage makes an excellent substitute.

Wash and scrub the artichokes very thoroughly but don't peel them. Then slice the artichokes across in thin slices. Cut just the base off the Chinese leaf, then slice it across very thinly. Cut the chilli open lengthways under running water, discard the seeds and stem and then slice the flesh across as thinly as you possibly can. Chop the flat leaf parsley.

Put the butter and both the sunflower and sesame oils in a wok or a large, deep frying pan over a fairly high heat. Add the sliced artichokes

and toss them with a large spoon for 3–4 minutes until they are softened but still slightly crunchy and holding their shape. Then add the chopped garlic and chilli and the sliced Chinese leaf. Stir the mixture for 1–2 minutes or until the Chinese leaf has become slightly limp. Finally, season with salt and a little black pepper and stir in the chopped parsley.

Turn the mixture into a heated serving dish. Sprinkle the dish with a little soy sauce and serve at once.
TO SERVE This dish can be used to great advantage if you want to provide some crunchy texture to a soft, creamy dish such as a savoury custard or cheese gratin.
Serves 4

SALADS

I once wrote a whole book on salads. I worked on it for several months and it was not until the depths of a cold winter that my family protested that they were rather tired of eating salads every day. And a fridgeful of limp, half-eaten salads became a bit depressing. So then I devised some more substantial salads using cooked or semi-cooked vegetables, and their interest revived. As in almost all dishes, the contrast of textures in a salad is one of the keys to its appeal. By using cooked vegetables too, you can exploit those mellow flavours which are absent before heat brings them out. Another effect which works well is to mix hot or warm ingredients with cold. Salads are aesthetically pleasing and of great nutritional value. On a hot summer's day, I enjoy

few meals more than a collection of different salads, carefully balanced. Several of the salads in this chapter can be combined to make a summer meal, or alternatively are ideal to serve as a starter for a more formal occasion. Some will make a light meal on their own, perfect for a quick lunch with a friend. One of the best things about salads is that you can actually feel that they are good for you; they have a refreshing effect on the stomach and hardly ever make you too full or sleepy. When my daughter lived in Russia for a year, she sometimes had nothing fresh and green to eat for weeks. We are very lucky indeed to have such a wealth of ingredients easily available, which enable us to create salads for all seasons that are endlessly interesting.

PEACH, ROCKET AND MIXED LEAF SALAD WITH
ROSE PETALS AND ROSE WATER DRESSING

This is the epitome of a pretty, romantic salad. Roses are not only decorative, but have a distinctive, tantalizing flavour too.

> *4 firm yellow-fleshed peaches*
> *4 tablespoons lemon juice*
> *Generous handful of rocket leaves*
> *3 handfuls of mixed salad leaves*
> *1 teaspoon pink peppercorns*
> *Petals of 2 pink roses*
> *FOR THE DRESSING:*
> *2 tablespoons lime juice*
> *3 tablespoons rose water*
> *4 tablespoons grapeseed or*
> *   sunflower oil*
> *3 pinches of chilli powder*
> *Sea salt and black pepper*

◀ *Peach, rocket and mixed leaf salad with rose petals and rose water dressing*

If the peaches are unblemished, they need not be skinned, unless you would prefer them peeled. If they do require skinning, put the peaches into a bowl, pour enough boiling water over them to cover them completely, and leave them for one or two minutes; then drain away the water and peel the peaches. Slice them finely in half-moon slices and then put them back into the empty bowl, together with the lemon juice. Stir lightly with a wooden spoon to coat the slices with the lemon juice.

Arrange the rocket leaves and a selection of pretty, varied salad leaves on a shallow serving dish or on six individual plates. Gently mix in the lemon-juice-coated peach slices. Crush the pink peppercorns roughly in a pestle and mortar, or by pressing down

on them in a pudding basin with the back of a large metal spoon. Sprinkle them over the salad. Finally, scatter the rose petals over the top of the salad.

Just before you serve the salad, put the lime juice, rose water, grapeseed or sunflower oil, chilli powder and sea salt and black pepper into a clean jam jar, seal with a lid and shake up vigorously. Taste the dressing for seasoning and adjust it to suit your individual taste.

Pour the dressing gently over the salad and serve.
TO SERVE You can serve this as a light first course or as an accompaniment to chicken or fish. Or it would make a beautiful centrepiece salad for a summer party.
Serves 6

SCALLOP SALAD WITH GRILLED YELLOW PEPPER AND MIXED FRESH HERBS

This is a warm and cold salad which can form the main course of a light lunch or supper because the steamed scallops are both rich and satisfying.

1 large yellow pepper
2 Little Gem lettuces or 1 small crisp lettuce
375g (12oz) tomatoes
5 tablespoons extra virgin olive oil
1 small garlic clove, chopped finely
2 tablespoons wine vinegar
1 tablespoon each fresh chopped fennel, dill or tarragon, or a mixture of all 3
500g (1lb) small queen scallops or 6–8 large scallops
½ tablespoon fresh mint leaves, roughly chopped
FOR THE VINAIGRETTE DRESSING:
4 tablespoons extra virgin olive oil
1 tablespoon wine vinegar
Salt and black pepper

First cut the pepper in half, discard the seeds and stem and put the two halves, skin side up, under a very hot grill. Leave the pepper halves under the grill until the skins are really blackened in patches, then put them into a plastic or paper bag and leave on one side until they are cool enough to handle.

Meanwhile, arrange the lettuce leaves on a large round shallow serving dish. Cut the tomatoes across in rounds and arrange the slices on top of the lettuce leaves. Then take the pepper halves out of the plastic bag and peel off the skin. Cut the flesh up into long strips and arrange the strips on top of the tomatoes and lettuce.

To make the vinaigrette dressing, place the oil and vinegar together in a clean jam-jar. Season to taste, cover with a lid and shake the jar vigorously.

Pour the five tablespoons of olive oil into a large saucepan or sauté pan and heat gently. Then add the chopped garlic and stir over the heat for 30 seconds. Add the vinegar and season with salt and black pepper; then stir in the fennel, dill and tarragon and remove the pan from the heat.

Bring a little water to the boil in the bottom of a steamer, put the scallops in the top of the steamer and steam for about two minutes only, or just until they turn opaque and become slightly firmer. Do not overcook them, as they will become tough and rubbery.

Add the scallops to the warmed dressing in the saucepan and mix gently with a wooden spoon. Shortly before eating, shake the vinaigrette dressing up again and spoon it over the salad. Lastly, transfer the scallops and their juices to the centre of the salad, sprinkle with the roughly chopped mint and serve immediately.
Serves 4

DELICATELY SPICED POTATO AND PRAWN SALAD WITH SOURED CREAM AND FRESH DILL

Fresh dill is a wonderful complement to both potato and prawns. All three flavours meld together perfectly in this quickly made salad for a delicious light meal. Allow enough time for the potatoes to cool down when you make this.

625g (1¼lb) small waxy new potatoes
3 tablespoons extra virgin olive oil
2 large garlic cloves, chopped very finely
2 teaspoons ground coriander
1 teaspoon ground cardamom
300g (10oz) large peeled prawns
300ml (½ pint) soured cream or creamed smetana
Generous handful of fresh dill, chopped finely
3–5 pinches of chilli powder
Salt
Fresh dill, to garnish

◄ *Scallop salad with grilled yellow pepper and mixed fresh herbs.*

Scrub the potatoes well but don't peel them. Cut the potatoes in half, or quarters if necessary. Then steam or boil the potatoes until they are just cooked.

Meanwhile, put the olive oil into a small frying pan over a low heat. Add the chopped garlic and the ground coriander and cardamom and stir for about four minutes. Remove the pan from the heat. When the potatoes are cooked, drain and put them into a mixing bowl with the peeled prawns. Pour the oil, garlic and spices from the frying pan into the hot potato and prawn mixture. Mix together with a wooden spoon and leave until cool.

Put the soured cream into a bowl. Mix in the chopped dill and add chilli powder and salt to taste. Now pour this dressing on to the cooled potatoes and prawns. Mix in the dressing gently and spoon the salad on to a serving dish. Garnish the edge of the dish with a few sprigs of fresh dill.

TO SERVE Accompany by a generous salad of mixed red and green leaves and fresh herbs.
Serves 4

▲ *Delicately spiced potato and prawn salad with soured cream and fresh dill*

SPICED CHICKEN LIVER SALAD
WITH FRESH MINT AND PINE KERNELS

Warm salads are perfect for a quick-to-prepare, light meal. This dish has a somewhat Middle Eastern character to it. The combination of textures with the warm, spicy chicken livers and the crisp salad leaves is truly delicious.

3 tablespoons grapeseed or
   groundnut oil
3 tablespoons walnut or hazelnut oil
2 teaspoons ground paprika
2 teaspoons ground cinnamon
1 rounded teaspoon cumin seeds
1 rounded teaspoon caster sugar
3–4 pinches of chilli powder
500g (1lb) chicken livers
1 small frisée lettuce
Generous handful of fresh mint
   leaves
25g (1oz) pine kernels
1 large garlic clove, chopped finely
2 tablespoons sherry vinegar
1 tablespoon soy sauce
Salt

Put the oils into a mixing bowl and stir in the ground paprika and cinnamon, the cumin seeds, the caster sugar and the chilli powder. Then add the chicken livers and stir them around with a wooden spoon to coat them thoroughly with the oil and spice mixture.

Separate the frisée leaves. Wash them under cold running water and dry them fairly thoroughly using a salad spinner or by gently patting them dry with kitchen paper or a clean tea towel.

Place the frisée leaves in a large salad bowl. Add the fresh mint leaves and mix up the salad well to ensure that the mint is thoroughly distributed. Place a large sauté pan (or, if you have one, you can use a wok) over a medium heat, add the pine kernels and stir them around in the dry sauté pan until they begin to turn a golden brown colour. Then add the chicken liver mixture, together with all its oil and spices, and stir for only 5–6 minutes –

this should be just long enough to cook the chicken livers while still keeping them slightly pink inside. Add the chopped garlic and continue to stir for another 30 seconds. Finally, add the sherry vinegar, the soy sauce and a sprinkling of salt. Stir the contents of the pan again just to mix, then remove the pan from the heat.

Spoon the chicken livers on top of the frisée and mint salad, then pour the oil and juices from the pan all over the leaves and serve the salad at once while the chicken livers are still warm but the leaves are still crisp.
TO SERVE Good bread is a natural partner to any dish which leaves wonderful, spicy oils on the plate. An open-textured white bread such as Italian ciabatta is ideal. In any event, this works very well as one of several salads to make up a meal, but it also makes an excellent starter.
Serves 4

JERUSALEM ARTICHOKE AND AVOCADO SALAD
WITH VINAIGRETTE DRESSING

The two nutty, subtle flavours of the jerusalem artichoke and avocado pear complement each other well to make this simple first course, as do their different textures. The salad is enlivened by green peppercorns, and dressed with a simple vinaigrette dressing of extra virgin olive oil and wine vinegar.

4 tablespoons lemon juice plus a
   little extra
500g (1lb) jerusalem artichokes
2 avocados
1 teaspoon bottled green
   peppercorns
Generous handful of parsley,
   chopped finely
FOR THE VINAIGRETTE DRESSING:
4 tablespoons extra virgin olive oil
1 tablespoon wine vinegar
Salt and pepper

◀ *Spiced chicken liver salad with fresh mint and pine kernels*

Put the four tablespoons lemon juice into a small saucepan of salted water. Scrub the artichokes thoroughly but don't peel them. Then slice the artichokes across very thinly and drop them into the salted water. Bring the water to the boil and allow it to bubble for 3–4 minutes, just until the artichokes are lightly cooked but still crunchy. Drain the artichokes and set them aside. Shortly before serving, slice the avocados in half, remove the stone, then peel off the skin. Slice the flesh thinly across in half circles, sprinkling them with lemon juice as you go. To assemble the dish, place the artichoke slices on a shallow serving plate or on to individual serving plates, and simply arrange the avocado slices on top. Sprinkle over the green peppercorns. Prepare the vinaigrette by putting all the ingredients into a sealed jar and shaking it well to combine. Just before serving, spoon the vinaigrette

dressing evenly all over the artichoke and avocado slices and sprinkle the dish with finely chopped parsley.
Serves 4

▲ *Jerusalem artichoke and avocado salad with vinaigrette dressing*

POACHED QUAILS' EGGS WITH SPINACH AND PINE KERNELS

You need really fresh quails' eggs for poaching, otherwise they will break up in the water.

25g (1oz) pine kernels
Dash of white wine vinegar
12 quails' eggs
1.1kg (2½lb) fresh spinach, trimmed
75g (3oz) butter
¼–½ whole nutmeg, grated
1 radicchio
1 tablespoon balsamic vinegar
3–4 tablespoons olive oil
Salt and black pepper

Put a small, dry frying pan over a high heat. Tip in the pine kernels and stir for 1–2 minutes, until they are just toasted. Leave to one side on a plate. Put some water in a wide shallow saucepan and add the white wine vinegar. Bring the water up to a fierce boil and carefully break in the eggs so as not to break the yolks. Poach them for less than one minute, just until the white is opaque and the yolk has lost its transparent gloss – the yolk should still be runny inside. Carefully lift out the eggs with a slotted spatula and leave on one side.

Shortly before your meal, cook the spinach in salted water for a few minutes until soft. Drain the spinach and press out as much liquid as possible. Now put the spinach into a food processor with the butter and nutmeg and whizz to a smooth purée. Season to taste. Arrange the eggs, spinach purée, pine kernels and radicchio leaves on individual plates. Sprinkle the eggs with salt and black pepper. Just before serving, dribble the balsamic vinegar and oil on top.
Serves 4

EGGS WITH TOMATO AND BASIL MAYONNAISE

The sublime combination of tomatoes and basil is the epitome of summer. The fresher the eggs the creamier their whites will be. This is perfect as part of a cold 'al fresco' lunch on a warm day.

8 large very fresh eggs (size 1)
2 ripe tomatoes
2 egg yolks
1 garlic clove, chopped roughly
1 tablespoon tomato purée
300ml (½ pint) olive oil
12–15 fresh basil leaves, sliced
Salt
Black pepper
Fresh basil, to garnish

Put the eggs into a saucepan, cover with cold water and bring to the boil. Boil the eggs for four minutes — this should give you semi-hard boiled eggs with the yolks darker and softer in the middle. As soon as they are cooked, cool the eggs under cold running water. Then peel them, halve lengthways and arrange the slices fanning outwards in a shallow round dish.

To make the mayonnaise, put the tomatoes in a bowl and cover them with boiling water. Remove the tomatoes after one minute and peel. Put the peeled tomatoes into a food processor with the egg yolks, the

chopped garlic and the tomato purée. Whizz the mixture until smooth. Then, with the machine running, add the oil, drop by drop at first, and then in a thin stream until the mixture reaches the right thickness.

Add salt and pepper to taste. Add the sliced basil leaves to the mayonnaise and whizz briefly to mix. Spoon the mayonnaise over the eggs. Garnish with thinly sliced strips of fresh basil and eat as soon as possible.
TO SERVE Serve with several other cold dishes or warm or cold salads to make a delicious and varied meal.
Serves 4

GREEN SALAD WITH SPRING FLOWERS

Edible flowers add romance and beauty to food. This combination is wonderfully striking, with its vibrant colours.

2–3 Little Gem lettuces
Generous handful of edible flowers
   such as primroses or sweet violets
50g (2oz) fresh raspberries
1 tablespoon raspberry vinegar
5 tablespoons hazelnut oil
Salt
Black pepper

◄ *Poached quails' eggs with spinach and pine kernels; eggs with tomato and basil mayonnaise*

Pull the leaves of the lettuces apart, wash, dry and put into a salad bowl. Lightly mix in the edible flowers, together with their leaves if edible.

Press the raspberry flesh and juice through a sieve into a small bowl. Add the raspberry vinegar and hazelnut oil and stir very thoroughly with a fork.

Season to taste with salt and black pepper and dress the salad with the raspberry and hazelnut oil mixture just before serving.
TO SERVE You could serve this as part of a simple summer lunch, or as a spectacular party dish.
Serves 4

▲ *Green salad with spring flowers*

CHINESE SALAD
WITH BEAN SPROUTS AND CRISPY SPICED GARLIC

For lovers of garlic and crunchiness this salad is irresistible.

2 Little Gem lettuces
1 bunch of spring onions
250g (8oz) fresh bean sprouts
8–10 garlic cloves
2.5cm (1 inch) fresh root ginger
3 tablespoons groundnut oil
2 teaspoons Chinese 5-spice powder
FOR THE DRESSING:
2 tablespoons lemon juice
1½ tablespoons soy sauce
1 tablespoon clear honey
2 tablespoons sunflower oil
2 teaspoons sesame oil
3 pinches of chilli powder

Cut each lettuce into eight pieces lengthways and put the sections into a salad bowl. Cut the spring onions across into 5mm (¼-inch) slices, using as much of the green part as possible. Mix the spring onions and the bean sprouts with the lettuces.

Chop the garlic cloves finely and thinly slice the fresh root ginger. Put the groundnut oil into a frying pan over a medium heat. Add the chopped garlic and stir constantly for about two minutes or until the garlic is browned and crisp – watch it carefully so that it doesn't burn. Then add the Chinese five-spice powder and the sliced ginger. Stir for 30 seconds and remove

the pan from the heat. Leave on one side to cool for a few minutes.

To make the dressing, simply put all the ingredients into a jam jar. Cover the jar and shake thoroughly. Just before you eat, shake the jar again and pour the dressing on to the salad. Pour the sliced garlic and ginger mixture over the top. Toss the salad to mix in the dressing and serve immediately.
TO SERVE This spicy salad makes the perfect accompaniment to cold roast chicken or poached fish. It should be prepared no more than 20 minutes before you plan to eat to preserve its crunchy freshness.
Serves 4–5

EXOTIC EGG AND CUCUMBER SALAD
WITH COCONUT AND YOGURT SAUCE

Oriental flavours, such as ginger, cardamom and coconut, combine well with more conventional ingredients to make tasty and original salads. This is a lovely light salad, with a subtly flavoured spicy sauce. It is especially good when accompanied by hot steamed or boiled new potatoes for an informal lunch.

2 fresh red or green chillies
2.5cm (1-inch) piece of fresh root
    ginger, chopped roughly
2 garlic cloves, chopped roughly
4–5 green cardamom pods, crushed
    lightly
300ml (½ pint) milk
50g (2oz) instant coconut milk
    powder or 125g (4oz) creamed
    coconut, crumbled
6 large eggs (size 1)
½ large cucumber
1 Cos or other crisp lettuce
Handful of fresh mint leaves,
    chopped finely
150g (5oz) Greek-style yogurt
Generous handful of fresh coriander
    leaves
Salt

◄ Chinese salad with bean sprouts and crispy spiced garlic

Cut the chillies open under running water, discard the seeds and stem and chop the flesh up roughly. Put the chilli, ginger, garlic and crushed cardamom into a saucepan with the milk and a sprinkling of salt. Bring this to the boil and simmer very gently, stirring now and then, for 10 minutes. Remove the pan from the heat. Stir in the coconut milk powder or crumbled creamed coconut, and stir well until it has dissolved. Leave it to stand for about five minutes. Strain the warm milk into a bowl and leave until cold.

Meanwhile, put the eggs in a saucepan of cold water and bring to the boil. Bubble the water for one minute; then remove the pan from the heat and leave the eggs to cool in the water.

While the eggs are cooling, peel the cucumber and cut it into small cubes. Separate the lettuce leaves and cut them in half lengthways if they are large. Arrange the leaves in a shallow dish or on individual plates. Scatter the chopped mint over the lettuce leaves.

When the eggs are cold, peel and slice them across. Arrange the egg slices and cubed cucumber in the serving dish.

Stir the yogurt into the strained

cooled milk and taste to see if you need extra seasoning.

Chop the coriander leaves roughly, reserving one or two perfect sprigs for decoration. Stir the chopped leaves into the mixture.

Spoon the sauce on to the eggs and cucumber and decorate with the reserved whole coriander.
Serves 4

▲ Exotic egg and cucumber salad with coconut and yogurt sauce

CHICORY, AVOCADO, CHERRY TOMATO AND WALNUT SALAD

This is a simple salad with a very pleasant mixture of textures.

3 chicory
1 large avocado
Lemon juice, to sprinkle
300g (10oz) cherry tomatoes
50g (2oz) walnut pieces
FOR THE DRESSING:
150ml (¼ pint) creamed smetana or
    soured cream
2 tablespoons walnut oil
2 teaspoons caster sugar
1 bunch of fresh chives
Salt
Chilli powder, to taste

Cut off the bases of the chicory and separate the leaves. Arrange the leaves in one large, fairly shallow dish or on individual plates if you prefer.

Cut the avocado in half lengthways, remove the stone and then slice the flesh lengthways. Sprinkle the avocado pieces immediately with lemon juice so that they won't discolour. Arrange the avocado slices on the chicory leaves.

Slice the cherry tomatoes in half, and add them to the chicory and avocado. Liberally sprinkle the walnut pieces on to the salad.

To make the creamy dressing, put the smetana or soured cream into a bowl and thoroughly stir in the walnut oil and the caster sugar. Add salt and chilli powder to taste.

Hold the bunch of chives in one hand over the bowl containing the dressing mixture and, using scissors, snip off fairly small pieces. Mix the chives thoroughly into the dressing and then spoon the dressing roughly over the salad.

TO SERVE This versatile salad can be served as a first course on its own or as an accompaniment to grilled chicken or fish. The dressing can also be used successfully for other salads.
Serves 4–5

SLICED WATERMELON, RED ONION AND WATERCRESS SALAD

The crisp and slightly sweet flavour of watermelon makes it an ideal vehicle for salad dressings. This is a decorative and refreshing salad.

750g–1kg (1½–2lb) watermelon
2 small red onions
4 tablespoons lemon juice
6 tablespoons extra virgin olive oil
1 bunch of watercress leaves
Salt and black pepper
Paprika, to sprinkle

Thinly slice the watermelon in medium-sized pieces, removing any pips. Remove the peel from the slices. Lay the watermelon slices in a shallow dish or roasting tin lined with kitchen paper. Slice the onions as thinly as possible into rings. Lay the onion rings on top of the watermelon slices. Cover the tin with clingfilm and leave for 30 minutes. Put the lemon juice, olive oil and a generous seasoning of salt and black pepper into a jam jar.

Remove the slices of watermelon and arrange them on individual plates with the onion rings and watercress leaves.

TO SERVE Just before serving, shake the lemon dressing up vigorously in the jam jar and spoon it over the watermelon slices. Lastly, sprinkle each serving with a very little paprika. This goes well with smoked salmon or other cured or cold fish.
Serves 6

SPICY CHICKEN AND FRISÉE SALAD

This quick-to-prepare hot and cold salad has Chinese undertones.

2 skinless chicken breast fillets
1 cinnamon stick
2 tablespoons groundnut oil
2 tablespoons walnut oil
2 teaspoons paprika
1 teaspoon allspice
1 rounded teaspoon caster sugar
3–4 pinches of chilli powder
1 large frisée
3 small red onions
1 tablespoon wine vinegar
1 tablespoon soy sauce
Salt

Slice the chicken breasts across very finely. Grind the cinnamon stick very finely in a coffee grinder or pestle and mortar. Put the groundnut oil and walnut oil, the paprika, the ground cinnamon and the allspice, the caster sugar and chilli powder into a medium-sized mixing bowl. Stir to mix. Then stir the sliced chicken breasts into this mixture and leave it for a few minutes to absorb the flavours.

Wash and separate the frisée. Slice the red onions thinly and place them, together with the frisée leaves, in a fairly large salad bowl.

Heat a dry frying pan or a wok over a medium heat. Add the chicken breast mixture and toss around for only 4–5 minutes, just until the chicken is opaque. Then stir in the vinegar, the soy sauce and a sprinkling of salt. Remove the pan from the heat.

Spoon the chicken mixture into the salad bowl of frisée and onions. Pour the pan juices over the salad and mix lightly. Serve at once.
Serves 4

▶ Chicory, avocado, cherry tomato and walnut salad; sliced watermelon, red onion and watercress salad; spicy chicken and frisée salad

68

JAMIE'S CIABATTA BREAD SALAD
WITH ORANGES AND RED ONIONS

A friend of mine makes this delicious Italian-style salad which is substantial enough as a light lunch on its own or accompanied by mozzarella cheese. If possible, use ciabatta bread which is a day or two old, as it absorbs the olive oil better. This salad can be made at least an hour in advance.

2 yellow peppers
1 red pepper
300ml (½ pint) extra virgin olive oil
  (approximately)
3 large garlic cloves, sliced thinly
3 small oranges
4 very ripe tomatoes
2 small red onions, sliced finely
8–10 fresh basil leaves
¾ ciabatta loaf
Salt and black pepper

Cut the peppers in half lengthways, discard the seeds and stem and slice across the flesh as finely as you can.

Put 150ml (¼ pint) of the olive oil in a large, deep frying pan over a low heat. Add the sliced peppers and cook them very gently until just becoming soft; then add the sliced garlic and continue cooking gently, stirring often, until the peppers are really soft. Remove the pan from the heat and leave on one side.

Peel the oranges, remove the pith and then pull off the thin skin from each of the segments. Put the skinned segments into a mixing bowl.

Put the tomatoes into another bowl and pour enough boiling water over them completely to cover them. Leave the tomatoes for one minute, then peel them and slice the flesh. Add the sliced tomatoes to the orange segments in the mixing bowl.

Add the onion slices to the oranges and the tomatoes. Mix the basil leaves in with the tomatoes, oranges and onion slices, either whole or just torn roughly if you prefer.

Cut the bread in slices and then across into roughly 2.5cm (1-inch) cubes. Put the bread on top of the other ingredients in the bowl and then pour the remaining olive oil over the bread, allowing it to absorb.

Finally, tip in the contents of the frying pan and mix all the ingredients together. Season with salt and plenty of black pepper. Turn the salad into a serving bowl to serve.
Serves 4

WILD RICE SALAD
WITH CUCUMBER AND FRESH ORANGE

To me, rice salads often seem very dull. But wild rice – which isn't really rice but a type of grass – has nutty-flavoured, chewy-textured black grains which make it perfect for eating cold. Adding the dressing while the rice is hot means that the rice absorbs the flavours and moisture of the dressing much more effectively. This is an easy salad for a party as it can be prepared in advance.

250g (8oz) wild rice
750ml (1¼ pints) water
1 red pepper
1 yellow or orange pepper
½ large cucumber
1 small orange
1 small garlic clove
1½ tablespoons sherry vinegar
6 tablespoons extra virgin olive oil
1 small red onion, chopped very
  finely
2 handfuls of flat leaf parsley
Sea salt
Black pepper

Put the wild rice into a saucepan with the water and bring it to the boil. Stir, then cover the pan and simmer the rice very gently indeed for 40–45 minutes, or until the rice is soft but still with a slight bite to it. Uncover the saucepan for the last few minutes of cooking.

While the rice is cooking, prepare the vegetables and the vinaigrette dressing. Slice the peppers in half and discard the seeds and stem. Then chop the peppers finely. Turn the peppers into a large mixing bowl. Peel the cucumber and slice it thinly. Peel the orange, and remove the pith and the thin inner skin carefully. Using a very sharp knife, cut the orange flesh into cubes or chunks.

To make the dressing, press the garlic through a crusher into a jam jar. Add the sherry vinegar and the olive oil and season the mixture well with crushed sea salt and plenty of black pepper.

When the rice is ready, drain it and turn it into the bowl with the chopped peppers. Cover the jam jar, shake the dressing up vigorously, pour over the rice and mix in. Leave the rice until cold. Then mix in the chunks of fresh orange, the cucumber slices, the red onion and the sprigs of flat leaf parsley.
TO SERVE Turn the rice salad into a pretty serving bowl.
Serves 6

▲ *Wild rice salad with cucumber and fresh orange*

◀ *Jamie's ciabatta bread salad with oranges and red onions*

CARROT AND YOGURT SALAD
WITH PINE KERNELS AND STEAMED OKRA

This is a simple but pretty salad with interesting textures and Middle Eastern flavours. My impression is that organically grown carrots really do taste better, especially when raw. Make sure the okra are firm and unblemished.

175g (6oz) fresh okra
4 tablespoons lemon juice
4 tablespoons olive oil
25g (1oz) pine kernels
1 rounded teaspoon cumin seeds
5 rounded tablespoons Greek yogurt
2 teaspoons ground coriander
Generous handful of fresh mint
375g (12oz) carrots
Salt and black pepper
Sprigs of mint, to garnish

Remove just the top stem end off the okra, without piercing the pod, and put the okra in a steamer over boiling water. Cook for two minutes only, just until the okra turn bright green. Put the hot okra in a bowl, stir in the lemon juice and a little of the olive oil. Season with salt and black pepper and leave on one side until cool.

Put the remaining olive oil in a frying pan over a medium heat. Add the pine kernels and stir for one or two minutes just until they are browned in patches. Add the cumin seeds and stir for 30 seconds. Remove the pan from the heat and leave to one side.

Put the yogurt into another bowl and stir in the ground coriander. Chop the mint leaves finely and add them to the mixture together with a good seasoning of salt and black pepper. Peel or scrub the carrots and, using a fine paring knife or potato peeler, shave them into thin ribbons.

To assemble the salad, arrange the yogurt mixture, a tangle of carrot ribbons and the cooled okra in a large serving bowl or on individual plates. Spoon the oil, pine kernel and cumin seed dressing over the top. Garnish with sprigs of fresh mint.
TO SERVE This salad goes well as a side dish with cold chicken but it also makes a substantial main course served on its own.
Serves 4

CHICK PEA, FETA CHEESE AND TOMATO SALAD
WITH GREEN CHILLI AND LEMON DRESSING

Chick peas are one of the most popular of the pulses as they have lots of flavour and texture. They can hardly be overcooked. The time pulses take to cook depends on their age so you simply have to test them now and then until they are done. This is a satisfying salad which makes a good lunch simply accompanied by bread and perhaps a lettuce salad. Remember to leave plenty of time beforehand for the soaking of the chick peas.

175g (6oz) dried chick peas
1 fresh green chilli
1 small garlic clove
Juice and finely grated zest of
*   1 lemon*
7 tablespoons extra virgin olive oil
500g (1lb) well-flavoured ripe
*   tomatoes*
2 small red onions, sliced finely
175g–250g (6–8oz) feta cheese,
*   cubed*
8–10 fresh basil leaves
Sea salt
Black pepper

◀ *Carrot and yogurt salad with pine kernels and steamed okra*

Soak the chick peas for several hours, or overnight, in cold water. Then boil the chick peas in unsalted water for 30–45 minutes or until they are soft. Meanwhile, cut the chilli open under running water, discard the seeds and stem and chop up the flesh finely. Put the chilli into a jam jar.

Crush the garlic and add it to the jam jar. Add the lemon juice and zest and the olive oil, and season well with crushed sea salt and a little black pepper. Put a lid on the jam jar, shake up the ingredients together thoroughly and leave on one side.

When the chick peas are cooked, drain and put them into a mixing bowl. Shake up the dressing once more, pour it over the hot chick peas and mix together well. Leave until the chick peas are completely cold.

Put the tomatoes into a large bowl and pour boiling water over to cover them. Leave the tomatoes for a moment, then peel them and cut the flesh into smallish pieces.

Add the tomatoes, onion and feta cheese to the cooked chick peas, then add the basil leaves to the bowl, whole or roughly torn. Mix the ingredients gently but thoroughly together.
TO SERVE Just before you plan to eat, turn the salad into a serving bowl and mix gently to distribute the dressing.
Serves 6

▲ *Chick pea, feta cheese and tomato salad with green chilli and lemon dressing*

FISH & SHELLFISH

One of the benefits of a childhood spent in various parts of the world was that I experienced all sorts of different tastes early on. Children will often only eat fish as fish fingers, but fish fingers were not even available in the countries we lived in. Instead, we had fresh fish and shellfish, cooked carefully and with inspiration as my mother was extremely interested in food. It was only later at an English boarding school that I had the first shock of badly cooked fish which has put many people off for life; fortunately, not me. Many people who call themselves vegetarians actually continue to eat fish. My oldest daughter, whose favourite meal as a young child was roast beef and Yorkshire pudding, suddenly announced at the age of eleven that she was a vegetarian, but luckily she never gave up eating fish. Fish is never a burden to the stomach, it takes well to all kinds of sauces and goes beautifully with most vegetables. Its texture can thrill the senses and its flavour reach the peak of delicacy. I don't think I could live without it.

STUFFED SALMON WITH MEDITERRANEAN SAUCE

Here a whole salmon is stuffed with a delicate smoked haddock mousse, baked, and then served with a lovely olive oil, lemon and wine sauce with tomatoes, shallots and fresh basil.

1.25–1.5kg (3–3½lb) salmon, gutted
250g (8oz) undyed smoked haddock
*   fillet*
4 tablespoons double cream
2 large egg whites (size 1)
1 rounded teaspoon pink
*   peppercorns*
2 teaspoons small capers
½ lemon or lime, sliced thinly
FOR THE SAUCE:
250g (8oz) ripe plum tomatoes
Zest and juice of 1 lemon
175–250ml (6–8 fl oz) extra virgin
*   olive oil*
4 shallots, sliced into fine strips
1 teaspoon caster sugar
6 tablespoons white wine
10–12 fresh basil leaves, chopped
*   finely*
Salt and black pepper
Sprigs of dill or fennel, to garnish

◄ *Stuffed salmon with Mediterranean sauce*

Wash the salmon and pat it dry with kitchen paper. Set the oven to preheat at Gas Mark 6/200°C/400°F. Roughly cut up the smoked haddock and put the pieces into a food processor with the cream and egg whites; whizz until the mixture is as smooth as possible. Turn the mixture into a bowl, season with salt and pepper and stir in the pink peppercorns and the capers. Lay a large sheet of foil on a flat surface and butter it generously. Put the salmon on to the foil and spoon the smoked haddock mixture into the body cavity, using wet hands to pat the outside smooth. Lay the lemon slices over the salmon. Wrap up the fish securely in the foil and lay it carefully on a flat baking sheet. Cook the fish in the centre of the preheated oven, for 40–45 minutes, then turn off the heat but leave the wrapped fish in the oven for a further 15–20 minutes.

While the fish is cooking, prepare the sauce. Put the tomatoes in a bowl, pour enough boiling water over to cover, and leave them for a minute or two; then peel and cut the tomatoes into small cubes. Coarsely grate the lemon, then squeeze out the juice and keep the zest and juice on one side. Spoon three tablespoons of the olive oil into a saucepan over a fairly low heat, add the sliced shallots and stir for a few minutes until they turn soft and translucent. Then add the lemon zest and juice, the caster sugar and the tomatoes, followed by the wine and the remaining olive oil. Season the sauce with salt and plenty of black pepper, bring the mixture just up to boiling point, then cover the pan and simmer very gently for about 10 minutes. Remove the pan from the heat.

When the fish is ready, unwrap it carefully and lever it on to a large heated serving plate with the help of the foil. Garnish the salmon with fresh dill or fennel. Reheat the sauce without allowing it to boil, then remove the sauce from the heat and stir in the chopped basil.
TO SERVE Pour the sauce in a separate bowl to spoon over the fish and vegetables. New potatoes and a lightly steamed vegetable such as broccoli or cauliflower are perfect accompaniments.
Serves 6

STUFFED FISH FILLETS WITH TARRAGON AND PINE KERNEL SAUCE

Almost any fish fillets can be used for this, but I prefer red mullet, sea bream or red snapper. As this dish needs some last-minute attention, it is best served for an informal supper.

> 250g (8oz) fresh asparagus tips
> (5–8cm/2–3 inches long)
> 25g (1oz) butter
> 2 teaspoons ground coriander
> 125g (4oz) shiitake or chestnut
> mushrooms, sliced thinly
> 6 fillets red mullet, red snapper or
> sea bream (1–1.05kg/2–2¼lb total
> weight)
> 125ml (4 fl oz) orange juice
> FOR THE SAUCE:
> 50g (2oz) pine kernels
> 50g (2oz) butter
> 1 rounded tablespoon plain flour
> 300ml (½ pint) milk
> 1 tablespoon sherry vinegar
> 3 egg yolks
> 2 tablespoons roughly chopped
> tarragon
> Salt and black pepper

Steam or boil the asparagus tips until they are just soft, then leave them on one side. Melt the butter in a frying pan over a medium heat, add the ground coriander and the mushrooms and stir for a few minutes until the mushrooms have softened. Then season the mixture with salt and black pepper and transfer to a plate to cool. Set the oven to preheat at Gas Mark 5/190°C/375°F.

Lay out the fish fillets skin side down. Divide the cooked asparagus into six piles and lay one pile across the centre of each fillet. Spoon the cooked mushrooms on top. Bring up the sides of the fillets to enclose the filling in a loose roll and lay the rolls, join side down, in a fairly shallow, rectangular ovenproof dish. Put a generous knob of butter on top of each fillet and pour the orange juice into the dish around them. Cover the dish with foil. Cook the dish just above the centre of the preheated oven for 30–35 minutes; then turn off the oven and leave the door slightly open while you make the sauce.

To make the sauce, put a dry frying pan over a high heat, add the pine kernels and toss them around for 1–2 minutes until browned. Put the pan on one side. Melt the butter in a heavy-based saucepan over a medium heat. Remove the pan from the heat and stir in the flour until smooth. Gradually stir in the milk and the sherry vinegar. Put the pan back over the heat and bring back to the boil, stirring all the time. Continue stirring until the mixture is thickened. Pour in all the juices from the fish and bring the sauce back to the boil once again, stirring. Now add the egg yolks and stir over the heat for 2–3 minutes without boiling. Finally stir in the tarragon and the toasted pine kernels and season the sauce to taste with salt and black pepper.

TO SERVE Just before serving, pour the tarragon and pine kernel sauce over the stuffed fish fillets, either in their serving dish or on individual plates. Serve with new potatoes and spinach.
Serves 6

SALMON AND PRAWN SAUSAGES WITH PARSLEY AND PRAWN SAUCE

These poached 'sausages' can be kept warm for up to 30 minutes in a very low oven. The sauce can be gently reheated if necessary, stirring continuously.

> FOR THE SAUSAGES:
> 375g (12oz) skinned salmon fillet
> 125g (4oz) peeled prawns
> 2 large egg whites (size 1)
> 15g (½oz) cornflour
> 1 teaspoon baking powder
> 2 teaspoons pink peppercorns or
> 1 teaspoon bottled green
> peppercorns
> Finely grated zest of 1 orange
> Salt and black pepper
> FOR THE SAUCE:
> 200g (7oz) flat leaf parsley
> 50g (2oz) butter
> 25g (1oz) cornflour
> 450ml (¾ pint) vegetable stock
> 2 large egg yolks (size 1)
> 125g (4oz) peeled prawns
> Salt and black pepper

To prepare the sausages, put the salmon and prawns into a food processor with the egg whites, cornflour and baking powder. Season well with salt and black pepper and whizz until the mixture is smooth and pasty. Turn the mixture into a bowl and stir in the peppercorns and the orange zest. Using wet hands, mould the mixture into small, fat sausages. Bring a large saucepan of water up to a rolling boil. Simmer the sausages gently for eight minutes. Drain them carefully in a strainer, and put them in one layer in a lightly buttered, shallow oven-proof dish. Cover the dish only lightly with foil so that steam can escape. Keep the dish warm in a very low oven.

Meanwhile, make the sauce. Remove any thick stalks from the parsley and leave a few good sprigs to one side to use as a garnish. Put the parsley into a food processor and whizz as finely as possible. Melt the

butter gently in a heavy saucepan, remove from the heat and, using a wooden spoon, stir in the cornflour until smooth. Then stir in the vegetable stock. Put the saucepan back on the heat and bring to the boil, stirring all the time for 2–3 minutes or until the sauce is thickened and smooth. Now add the puréed parsley and stir over the heat for a further two minutes. Reduce the heat to low, add the egg yolks and stir for one minute. Lastly add the prawns and remove the pan from the heat. Season the sauce to taste with salt and pepper, if necessary.

TO SERVE Pour the sauce over the fish sausages and garnish with parsley. Serve with baby corn or baby carrots and new potatoes.
Serves 4

▶ *Stuffed fish fillets with tarragon and pine kernel sauce; salmon and prawn sausages with parsley and prawn sauce*

SALMON AND SWEETCORN PIE

A few strips of Thai lime leaves make this very easy pie even more delicious.

375g (12oz) skinless salmon fillet
2–3 sticks of lemon grass
1 fresh red chilli
5cm (2-inch) piece of root ginger, chopped finely
125g (4oz) frozen sweetcorn, thawed and blanched
Finely grated zest of 1 lemon
25g (1oz) coconut milk powder or 50g (2oz) creamed coconut
2 tablespoons very hot water
25g (1oz) butter
375g (12oz) ready-made puff pastry
1 beaten egg yolk plus a little milk, for glazing
Salt

Cut the salmon into 1cm (½-inch) cubes and put the pieces into a mixing bowl. Top and tail the lemon grass, removing any tough outer leaf, and slice the stems very finely across. Cut the chilli open lengthways under running water, discard the seeds and stem, then cut the flesh across into strips as thinly as you can. Add the chilli, lemon grass and ginger to the salmon, then gently mix in the sweetcorn, lemon zest and salt to taste. Blend the coconut milk powder or cream with the water, and add this to the salmon mixture. Finally, melt the butter and stir into the salmon mixture.

Set the oven to preheat at Gas Mark 7/220°C/425°F. Divide the pastry equally in two. Roll each into a fairly thin circle on a cool flat surface. Butter a flat baking sheet or a 25cm (10-inch) circular flan tin. Lay one circle of pastry on the baking sheet and pile the pie filling on to it, leaving 2.5cm (1 inch) around the edge uncovered. Moisten this edge with water and lay the second circle on top. Seal the edges and trim neatly, rolling out the trimmings to make decorations. Moisten these with a little water before placing them on the pie. Pierce two holes in the top of the pastry to allow the steam to escape. Glaze the pie with the mixture of egg yolk and milk. Cook the pie in the centre of the preheated oven for 25–35 minutes or until the pastry is a rich golden brown. Serve immediately.
Serves 4

LIGHT TUNA CAKES WITH TOMATO, PEPPER AND OLIVE OIL SAUCE

These light fish cakes can be made ahead of time and kept warm in a low oven until you are ready to eat.

FOR THE CAKES:
600ml (1 pint) milk
1 rounded teaspoon dried oregano
150g (5oz) fine semolina
25g (1oz) butter
75g (3oz) grated Cheddar cheese
1 large egg (size 1)
200g (7oz) can of light meat tuna, drained and mashed
Grated Parmesan, to sprinkle
FOR THE SAUCE:
1 large red pepper
375g (12oz) tomatoes
5 tablespoons extra virgin olive oil
4 tablespoons water
2 large garlic cloves, chopped finely
Salt and black pepper
Basil and parsley, to garnish

Put the milk, oregano and semolina into a saucepan, and season with salt and pepper. Stirring all the time, bring the mixture to the boil, and allow it to bubble for 2–3 minutes until it is very thick. Add the butter and Cheddar cheese, then turn the mixture into a bowl. Add the egg, lightly whisked, to the mixture, followed by the tuna. Allow to cool a little, cover and then refrigerate until completely cold.

Meanwhile, for the sauce, halve the pepper and discard the seeds and stem. Place the halves skin side upwards under a very hot grill until the skins are black, then put them into a plastic bag and leave on one side. Put the tomatoes into a bowl, and cover them with boiling water. Leave for 1–2 minutes, then drain, peel and chop the tomatoes. Put the oil and water into a pan, add the tomatoes and garlic and place over a moderate heat allowing the mixture to bubble very gently. Meanwhile, peel and chop the peppers and add them to the tomatoes. Continue bubbling gently for 10 minutes. Finally, remove from the heat.

When the semolina mixture is really cold, make the cakes. Oil a large shallow dish. Then, with lightly oiled hands, form the mixture into golfball-sized cakes. Place the balls slightly apart in one layer on the dish, and put them under a very hot grill for a few minutes until golden brown. Then turn them over, sprinkle with Parmesan and place under the grill again until brown.
TO SERVE Reheat the sauce and spoon it over the cakes. Garnish with basil and parsley leaves.
Serves 4

▲ *Light tuna cakes with tomato, pepper and olive oil sauce*

◀ *Salmon and sweetcorn pie*

SALMON AND LETTUCE RING

Pink and green is one of my favourite colour combinations, especially when they taste as good as this simple salmon mousse wrapped up in lettuce leaves. Because of its attractive appearance, this makes a perfect first course or buffet party dish, or you could serve it as the main course for a light but elegant summer lunch.

*1–2 round or Cos lettuces
  (depending on size), separated
  into leaves*
750g (1½lb) salmon
2 tablespoons hot water
*4 teaspoons powdered gelatine or
  2 teaspoons agar-agar flakes*
2 large eggs (size 1), separated
*2 tablespoons freshly squeezed
  lemon juice*
5 tablespoons double cream
2–4 pinches of chilli powder
Salt
*Sprigs of fennel or dill leaves, to
  garnish*

Generously smear a 1.2-litre (2-pint) ring-mould tin with olive oil. Bring a saucepan of salted water to the boil and then plunge in the separated lettuce leaves just until they turn limp. Drain the leaves well in a strainer by pressing down with the back of a wooden spoon to squeeze out the water, but take care not to tear the leaves, as they will be used to wrap the mousse mixture. Leave the lettuce on one side to cool. Either steam or poach the salmon until lightly cooked, then remove all the skin and bones and put the boneless flesh into a food processor. Put the hot water into a cup or bowl set over a pan of very hot but not boiling water, sprinkle in the gelatine or agar-agar and ensure that it has thoroughly dissolved, referring to the instructions on the packet if necessary. Add the gelatine and the egg yolks to the salmon and whizz to a purée. Add the lemon juice and cream and whizz the mixture again until very smooth, then add a little salt

and chilli powder to taste.

Line the prepared mould with the blanched lettuce leaves, bringing them up the sides so that they hang well over the edge. Now add a pinch of salt to the egg whites in a clean bowl and whisk until they stand in soft peaks. Using a metal spoon, fold the egg whites gently into the salmon mixture and then turn the mixture into the leaf-lined tin. Bring the lettuce leaves up over the salmon to enclose the filling, laying on extra leaves to fill in any gaps. Put the mousse in the refrigerator for about two hours until set.

Before serving, turn the ring out by turning it upside down on a serving plate and giving it a good shake. Garnish the mousse with sprigs of fresh herbs such as fennel or dill.
TO SERVE Use a very sharp knife to cut the ring into thick slices and serve with a bowl of homemade mayonnaise or Greek yogurt.
Serves 6–8

LIGHTLY POACHED MONKFISH IN CREAMY TARRAGON SAUCE

A poached fish with a very light, creamy tarragon sauce produces a simple but sophisticated dish that would be just right for a light lunch or supper. Because of its firm flesh, monkfish is easier to cook than softer fish but this recipe is also perfect for filleted sea bass. Use larger pieces of bass fillet than monkfish, with the skin still on.

1kg (2lb) filleted monkfish
4 tablespoons lemon juice
450ml (¾ pint) fish or chicken stock
150ml (¼ pint) white wine
150ml (¼ pint) double cream
*1 tablespoon chopped fresh
  tarragon leaves*
Salt
Black pepper
*Generous handful of fresh tarragon
  leaves, to garnish*

◄ *Salmon and lettuce ring; lightly poached
monkfish in creamy tarragon sauce*

Slice the fish into 2cm (¾-inch) slices. Place the fish slices in the bottom of a large heavy saucepan. Add the lemon juice and sprinkle the fish with a little salt and black pepper. Leave the fish on one side for a moment. Put the fish or chicken stock with the wine into a separate saucepan and bring this mixture to the boil. Then pour it over the fish. Place the fish over the heat and bring up to the boil again. The moment boiling point is reached, cover the pan with a well-fitting lid, turn off the heat and leave the residual heat of the stock mixture to cook the fish for about eight minutes, or until the flesh of the fish has turned opaque.

Using a slotted spatula, transfer the poached fish to a heated shallow serving dish, reserving the poaching liquid in the pan for making the tarragon sauce. Cover the fish with foil and keep it in a warm place while you prepare the sauce.

To make the sauce, bring the reserved poaching liquid up to the boil and boil fiercely, uncovered and without stirring, for about 10 minutes, or until it has reduced to less than a quarter of its original volume and is thickish and syrupy. Stir in the cream and one tablespoon of chopped fresh tarragon leaves. Reduce the heat a little. Bring the sauce back to the boil, and allow it to bubble gently for about three minutes until it has thickened slightly. Pour the sauce over the poached fish in the serving dish, garnish with whole fresh tarragon leaves and serve immediately.
TO SERVE Simple accompaniments are better with creamy sauces; a few boiled new potatoes (without butter) and a green vegetable, such as perfectly fresh mange tout steamed just lightly to preserve their crispness, are perfect accompaniments.
Serves 4

FAR EASTERN FISH STEAKS WITH CHERRY TOMATOES AND BABY CORN

2 fresh red chillies
1 tablespoon sesame seed oil
2 large garlic cloves, chopped finely
5cm (2-inch) piece of fresh root
*   ginger, chopped finely*
4 fish steaks such as monkfish or cod
175g (6oz) cherry tomatoes
2 star anise, broken
2 sticks of lemon grass, sliced thinly
Grated zest of 1 lemon
50g (2oz) coconut milk powder or
*   125g (4oz) creamed coconut*
300ml (½ pint) boiling water
2 tablespoons lemon juice
250g (8oz) fresh baby corn
Small bunch of spring onions
Salt and black pepper
Chopped fresh coriander, to garnish

Cut the chillies open under running water, discard the seeds and stems, and cut the flesh across into very thin strips. Heat the sesame oil in a large casserole over a medium heat. Add the garlic and ginger and stir for one minute. Remove from the heat. Place the fish steaks, the whole cherry tomatoes and the star anise in the casserole and sprinkle with the sliced chilli, the lemon grass and the grated lemon zest.

Set the oven to preheat at Gas Mark 3/160°C/325°F. Mix the coconut powder or cream with the boiling water in a bowl until dissolved. Then add the lemon juice. Add one teaspoon of salt and pour the mixture into the casserole. Put the casserole over a medium heat until the juices are just bubbling, then cover the dish and place in the centre of the oven for 40–50 minutes or until the fish is just cooked through.

Meanwhile, steam or boil the baby corn until they are cooked but still have a slight bite to them. Trim the spring onions, and chop them crossways into 1cm (½-inch) pieces, using as much of the green part as possible.

When the fish has cooked, add the corn and spring onions to the casserole, cover again and put the casserole back in the oven for only five minutes. Season the juices if necessary. Just before serving, sprinkle the dish with the chopped coriander leaves.
Serves 4

COD WITH SORREL AND SPINACH PURÉE IN PUFF PASTRY PACKETS

Although it is straightforward to make, this type of dish always looks impressive. Choose the thickest fillets of cod that you can find, or you can use other white fish, salmon fillets or smoked cod or haddock. The individual pastry packets can be made up in advance and kept in the refrigerator. I like to serve the cod with baby carrots or a tomato salad and new potatoes. If you can't get sorrel, use just 750g (1½lb) spinach and add the juice of a lemon to the purée.

500g (1lb) sorrel leaves
500g (1lb) spinach
75g (3oz) butter
750g (1½lb) thick cod fillets, skinned
Finely grated zest of 1 orange
500g (1lb) ready-made puff pastry
1 egg yolk
Salt and black pepper
Sorrel or rocket leaves, to garnish

Plunge the sorrel and spinach into a large saucepan with a little salted boiling water, cover and cook the leaves for a few minutes just until they are soft. Drain very thoroughly in a strainer, pressing out all the liquid you

possibly can with the back of a spoon. Then purée the leaves in a food processor, together with the butter and a sprinkling of pepper and salt. Leave the mixture until completely cold.

Cut the fish into six equal pieces. Sprinkle the fish with pepper on both sides and pat all over with the orange zest. Roll out the pastry very thinly and cut out a piece big enough to wrap one piece of fish. Spread some of the cold purée in the middle of this pastry, then lay on a piece of fish and spread more purée on top. Moisten the edges of the pastry with a little water and wrap up the sandwich of purée and fish fairly loosely, lightly pressing the edges together to seal. Repeat this with the other pieces of fish, gathering up the cuttings of pastry and re-rolling them to wrap each piece of fish. Butter a large baking sheet and carefully place the packets of fish, join side down, on it. Roll out any pastry trimmings and cut out decorations for the top. Pierce a small hole in the top of each packet to allow steam to escape. Now leave the packets in the refrigerator until you are ready to start cooking.

Set the oven to preheat at Gas Mark 6/200°C/400°F. Mix the egg yolk with two teaspoons of cold water and a very little salt, and brush all over the pastry. Cook in the centre of the oven for 25–30 minutes until golden brown.
TO SERVE Transfer the packets on to individual warmed plates and garnish with a few sorrel or rocket leaves.
Serves 6

◀ *Far Eastern fish steaks with cherry tomatoes and baby corn*

▲ *Cod with sorrel and spinach purée in puff pastry packets*

COD AND CHICORY PIE

Cod is one of my favourite fish – the large, succulent flakes are exquisite. Another favourite of mine is fish pie, particularly this one which is light with a cheesy top of thread-like pasta.

> 750g (1½lb) thick cod fillet, skinned
> 6 chicory
> 125g (4oz) butter
> Juice of 1 orange
> 125g (4oz) egg vermicelli, angels' hair or tagliolini
> 450ml (¾ pint) fish stock
> Finely grated zest of ½ orange
> 2 rounded teaspoons fresh tarragon, chopped roughly
> 3 teaspoons cornflour
> 1 tablespoon water
> 25g (1oz) plain flour
> 600ml (1 pint) milk
> 50g (2oz) mature Cheddar cheese, grated
> 2 egg yolks
> 1 tablespoon grated Parmesan
> Salt and black pepper

Slice the cod into thick 2.5cm (1-inch) chunks. Cut the ends off the chicory and then cut each in half lengthways, or in quarters if very plump. Melt half the butter in a heavy saucepan, add the chicory with any loose outer leaves and the orange juice. Cover the pan and simmer gently for about 20 minutes or until the chicory is very soft. Remove the chicory with a slotted spoon and place in a large, shallow, ovenproof dish. Meanwhile, cook the pasta in boiling salted water for 2–4 minutes, depending on its size, or until the pasta is just soft but still has a bite to it. Drain the pasta in a large strainer, rinse it through with cold water and place it in a bowl. Mix in a little oil to keep the pasta separate and put to one side. Pour the fish stock into the pan with the butter and orange juice and bring the mixture up to bubbling; then add the fish, cover the pan and simmer very gently for a few minutes or until the cod is opaque but very lightly cooked. Remove the pan from the heat and, using a slotted spoon, remove the pieces of cod and arrange them among the chicory. Add the orange zest and tarragon to the fish liquid remaining in the saucepan.

Mix the cornflour in a cup with the water and, using a wooden spoon, stir it into the fish liquid. Return the saucepan to the heat and bring to the boil, stirring until thickened, then allow it to bubble, still stirring, for two minutes. Remove the pan from the heat, add salt and pepper to taste and pour the mixture over the chicory and cod in the dish. Scatter the drained pasta evenly over the top. Now melt the remaining butter in a smaller saucepan and stir in the flour with a wooden spoon. Add the milk slowly and bring to the boil, stirring, and allow the sauce to bubble gently, still stirring, for three minutes. Add the grated Cheddar cheese and stir until melted, then remove the pan from the heat and briskly stir in the egg yolks. Season to taste with salt and black pepper, pour the mixture evenly over the pasta and sprinkle with the grated Parmesan. Place the dish under a hot grill for a few minutes until speckled brown, thenplace the dish in a very low oven, Gas Mark ½/130°C/250°F, until you are ready to serve. The dish will remain fresh and moist for at least 30 minutes.
TO SERVE This is best served simply with a mixed leaf salad.
Serves 6

SMOKED FISH AND SESAME BALLS WITH TOMATO SAUCE

If possible, buy undyed smoked fish for this as it has a more delicate flavour.

> 250g (8oz) skinless smoked cod or haddock
> 2 small egg whites (size 5)
> 5 spring onions, sliced finely
> 75g (3oz) fresh white breadcrumbs
> 50g (2oz) cheese, grated finely
> 3–4 pinches of chilli powder
> 2 tablespoons sesame seeds
> Groundnut oil, for frying
> *FOR THE SAUCE:*
> 250g (8oz) carton 8% fat natural fromage frais
> 3 plum tomatoes
> Generous handful of flat leaf parsley
> 1 garlic clove, crushed
> Salt and black pepper

Using a sharp knife, cut up the fish roughly, then place the pieces in a food processor with the egg whites. Whizz until the mixture turns to a pasty consistency. Spoon this mixture into a separate bowl and mix in the spring onions with the breadcrumbs and cheese. Stir the mixture together thoroughly with a wooden spoon and season with the chilli powder and a little salt. Using damp hands, roll small quantities of the mixture into walnut-sized balls. Put the sesame seeds into a separate bowl and roll the fish balls in the seeds until they are covered.

To make the sauce, put the fromage frais into a bowl. Put the tomatoes in a separate bowl and pour over enough boiling water to cover. Leave the tomatoes for a minute or two, then drain, skin and chop them finely. Chop the parsley finely, reserving a little to garnish, and stir into the fromage frais with the chopped tomatoes and garlic. Season the sauce with salt and pepper and spoon it into a serving bowl.

To cook the fish balls, pour groundnut oil into the bottom of a large heavy frying pan to a depth of 5mm (¼ inch) and place over a medium heat. Add the fish balls and fry, turning them gently, until rich brown all over.

Place the fish balls into a serving dish. Garnish the sauce with the remaining parsley and serve it with the warm fish balls.
Serves 4

▶ *Cod and chicory pie; smoked fish and sesame balls with tomato sauce*

TROUT POACHED IN SAFFRON WINE AND OLIVE OIL WITH PARSLEY

This simply prepared dish has a lovely, delicate fusion of flavours. It is perfect summer food.

2 teaspoons bottled green
  peppercorns
1 teaspoon coriander seeds
Generous pinch of saffron strands
250ml (8 fl oz) white wine
1 teaspoon caster sugar
375g (12oz) firm tomatoes
2 handfuls of flat leaf parsley
4 trout, gutted but with the heads
  left on
125ml (4 fl oz) extra virgin olive oil
4 teaspoons balsamic vinegar
  (approximately)
Salt and black pepper
Chopped parsley, to garnish

Roughly crush the green peppercorns and the coriander seeds and put them into a bowl or jug with the saffron strands. Put the wine into a saucepan with the sugar and bring the wine just to the boil, then pour it immediately on to the peppercorn mixture. Leave the mixture to cool, stirring now and then to infuse the flavours.

Meanwhile, put the tomatoes into a bowl. Pour over enough boiling water to cover them, then peel and cut the flesh into 5mm (¼-inch) cubes. Leave the tomatoes on one side. Chop the parsley as finely as possible in a processor, and spoon the parsley into the gutted body cavities of the trout. Lay the trout in a shallow, rectangular ovenproof dish and set the oven to preheat at Gas Mark 6/200°C/400°F. Spoon the tomatoes all round each fish. When the wine has cooled add the olive oil to it, pour the mixture into the dish with the fish and cover the dish with foil. Put in the centre of the oven for 30–40 minutes, or until the fish have just cooked through to the bone, uncovering for about the last five minutes to crisp up the skin. Using a slotted spatula, very carefully lift out each fish and put them on to individual warmed plates. Season the juices with salt and black pepper to taste, and then spoon both the juices and tomatoes round each fish. Lastly, spoon a little balsamic vinegar on to the top of each fish, garnish with parsley and serve.
Serves 4

THE MAHARAJAH'S MUSSELS

This dish might have been cooked for a maharajah by a memsahib as it is rather Anglo-Indian in character. The rich flavour of both mussels and mushrooms go exceptionally well with traditional Indian spices. This can easily be served at a dinner party as you can prepare it in advance and simply reheat it at the last moment. If you cannot find fresh mussels use ready-cooked ones (but not those preserved in brine) and halve the weight.

1.75kg (4lb) fresh mussels
150ml (¼ pint) freshly squeezed
  orange juice
1 small red chilli
½ teaspoon whole cardamom pods
1 teaspoon coriander seeds
40g (1½oz) butter
½ teaspoon ground turmeric
2 small garlic cloves, chopped
  finely
2.5cm (1-inch) piece of fresh root
  ginger, chopped finely
40g (1½oz) plain flour
250g (8oz) sliced mushrooms
Small handful of fresh coriander
  leaves, chopped roughly

◀ *Trout poached in saffron wine and olive oil with parsley*

Wash the mussels thoroughly. Discard any which do not close when tapped. Put the orange juice into a very large saucepan. Cover the pan, bring the juice to the boil and add the mussels. Cover the pan again and keep it over a high heat, shaking for a few minutes until the mussels have opened. Remove the pan from the heat. Remove the mussels from the pan and put them on one side. Discard any mussels which remain closed. Strain the pan juices through a sieve into a bowl.

Cut the chilli open lengthways under running water, discard the seeds and stem and chop finely. Grind the cardamom pods and coriander seeds very finely. Melt the butter in a large casserole over a medium heat. Stir in the ground spices and turmeric. Then add the garlic, ginger and chilli and stir for one minute. Remove the pan from the heat and stir in the flour until the mixture is smooth. Stir in a little of the reserved mussel liquid and continue stirring in the remaining liquid slowly. Put the sauce over a high heat and bring the mixture to the boil, stirring all the time until it thickens. Simmer, still stirring, for three minutes. Then add the sliced mushrooms and simmer, stirring, for about five minutes until they are soft. Then add the mussels and simmer for one minute. Lastly, stir in the chopped coriander.
TO SERVE Serve with either plain boiled basmati rice or boiled potatoes and a green vegetable, such as spinach or spring greens.
Serves 4

▲ *The maharajah's mussels*

THAI-INSPIRED STEW OF SQUID AND SHIITAKE MUSHROOMS

If you are unable to get sour shrimp paste for this stew, use the juice of a second lemon and chilli powder to taste.

4 medium-sized plum tomatoes
300ml (½ pint) fish or chicken stock
Juice of 1 lemon
2.5cm (1-inch) piece of fresh ginger,
*   sliced thinly*
2 large garlic cloves, sliced thinly
2 rounded teaspoons Thai sour
*   shrimp paste*
2 rounded tablespoons instant
*   coconut milk powder*
250g (8oz) shiitake mushrooms,
*   sliced thinly*
1kg (2lb) small prepared squid
Generous handful of fresh coriander
Salt

Put the tomatoes into a bowl, pour over enough boiling water to cover and leave them for two minutes; then peel the tomatoes and cut them into small cubes. Pour the fish stock into a large casserole and add the lemon juice, tomato, ginger and garlic. Bring the mixture to the boil, stir in the shrimp paste and continue stirring until the paste is dissolved. Cover the dish and simmer the casserole juices gently for 15 minutes.

Meanwhile, put the coconut milk powder into a measuring jug, pour in about 150ml (¼ pint) of boiling water and stir until smooth. Stir the mixture into the casserole juices and bring to the boil again. Add the sliced mushrooms, cover the dish and simmer gently again for another 15 minutes. Meanwhile, slice the squid across in rings, keeping the tentacle part whole, and put to one side in the cool.

When the mushrooms have cooked, remove the casserole from the heat and leave to one side. Just before you plan to eat, reheat the casserole to boiling point and drop in the squid pieces.

Allow the casserole to bubble for one minute, then cover the dish, remove from the heat and leave for 8–10 minutes. Add a little salt, if necessary, and just before serving, stir in the chopped coriander leaves.
TO SERVE Serve with either Thai fragrant rice or basmati rice and a mixed leaf salad.
Serves 4

BABY SQUID STUFFED WITH SALMON AND SPINACH

I actually enjoy the process of cleaning squid and it's not as difficult or unpleasant as many people imagine. However, with the tiny ones, which are the most tender of all, it does take time, so it is a bonus nowadays that they can often be bought ready-prepared. In this dish, within the pure white flesh of the squid packets, the bright green spinach, perked up with orange zest and chilli, and the pink salmon create a pretty mosaic; the dill-flecked sauce is shiny and translucent.

375g (12oz) fresh spinach
250g (8oz) skinned salmon fillet
Finely grated zest and juice of
*   1 small orange (optional)*
3–4 pinches of chilli powder
500–625g (1–1¼lb) ready-prepared
*   baby squid*
150ml (¼ pint) white wine
FOR THE SAUCE:
1 rounded teaspoon arrowroot or
*   cornflour*
2 tablespoons water
2 teaspoons dill vinegar
Generous handful of fresh dill,
*   chopped*
Salt
Fresh dill, to garnish

Remove any thick stalks from the spinach. Bring a saucepan of salted water to the boil, add the spinach and boil for 1–2 minutes or until the leaves become limp, then drain the leaves well, pressing out as much liquid as possible. Chop the spinach fairly roughly and leave to cool. Slice the salmon fillet into small cubes. Mix the grated orange zest, if using, with the spinach and season to taste with the chilli powder.

Remove the tentacle part of the prepared squid. Take a small amount of the spinach and stick it down into the squid, pressing it well in with one finger. Then insert a piece of salmon and repeat the same again until the squid is stuffed almost full. Be careful not to overstuff the squid as it may contract when cooked. Lastly, stopper the stuffing by pressing the squid's tentacle part on top. Repeat the process with the other squid.

Strain the orange juice, if using, into a wide shallow saucepan or a deep sauté pan with a lid. Add the white wine, place the pan over the heat and bring the wine to simmering point. Carefully place the stuffed squid into the wine mixture, cover the pan and simmer very gently for only 1–2 minutes, or just until the squid flesh has turned an opaque white. Remove the pan from the heat, remove the squid carefully using a slotted spatula (reserving the liquid in the pan) and arrange the squid on a wide serving plate. Cover the squid loosely with foil and keep it warm in a very low oven while you make the sauce.

To make the sauce, mix the arrowroot or cornflour in a cup with the water and dill vinegar until smooth. Then stir this mixture into the reserved wine liquid in the pan and return to the heat. Bring the mixture up to bubbling, stirring all the time until thickened, then stir in the chopped dill and remove from the heat. If necessary, season the sauce with salt and a pinch or two of chilli powder. Pour the warm sauce over the squid just before serving, and garnish with fresh dill.
TO SERVE For a light meal, serve this low-fat but delectable dish with new potatoes and a mixed or tomato salad.
Serves 4

▶ *Thai-inspired stew of squid and shiitake mushrooms; baby squid stuffed with salmon and spinach*

POULTRY

With my predilection for exotic and aromatic ingredients, the range of poultry now available provides me with endless interesting possibilities. Chicken is often thought to be merely a vehicle for other ingredients. In fact, good chicken simply roasted is rarely disappointing, but the versatility of chicken means that chicken dishes need never be boring. It adapts to any number of flavours and virtually all cooking methods so it has to be one of the most reliable family foods around. And nowadays there are several different types of chicken to choose from. Free-range chickens, which have the freedom to roam outdoors and eat a varied diet, have always had a real flavour of their own. They are now easier to come by, as are succulent corn-fed chickens. For people who are on a low-fat diet, skinless chicken breast fillets cooked with vegetables to give them moisture and interest are a boon. They are also perfect for stir-frying or for making kebabs, and for dishes where the proportion of meat to vegetables is low. When I first tried guinea fowl, I thought it would taste quite gamey, but it is in fact a more delicate bird than chicken and is best with subtle sauces and seasonings. However, if you like a slightly gamey flavour, Barbary duck, which I have also included in this chapter, is to me ideal; it is less fatty than the ordinary commercially reared duck and has a flavour nearer to wild duck, though with much more flesh and succulence.

CHICKEN BREASTS AND SUN-DRIED TOMATOES WITH TARRAGON AND PAPRIKA SAUCE

The chicken breasts in this quickly made dish are thinly sliced and cooked with paprika and tarragon, both flavours well known to enhance chicken.

*5–6 skinless chicken breast fillets
    about 150g (5oz) each
8 tablespoons lemon juice
2 rounded teaspoons paprika
1 large garlic clove, crushed
1 tablespoon fresh tarragon
50g (2oz) unsalted butter
12–14 sun-dried tomatoes
300ml (½ pint) double cream
Salt
Chilli powder
Generous bunch of rocket leaves, to
    garnish*

◀ *Chicken breasts and sun-dried tomatoes
with tarragon and paprika sauce*

Slice the chicken breast fillets thinly across and place them in a bowl with the lemon juice, paprika and garlic. Chop the tarragon and add to the bowl. Stir the breast slices to coat them evenly with the mixture, then cover and leave to absorb the flavours at room temperature for 30 minutes.

Melt the butter in a large, deep, heavy-based frying pan over a fairly low heat. Add the chicken mixture and cook gently, stirring now and then, for 8–10 minutes. Meanwhile, slice each sun-dried tomato into 3–4 pieces – if you can get the ones in jars of oil, they are nice and soft.

Then, using a slotted spatula, transfer the chicken slices to a plate on one side. Bubble the pan juices up fiercely for two minutes to reduce them slightly, remove the pan from the heat and stir in the double cream. Bring the mixture back to the boil and boil, stirring, for about 2–3 minutes or until it has thickened slightly. Season to taste with salt and chilli powder, and then return the cooked chicken breasts to the sauce in the pan, together with the sun-dried tomatoes. Stir the chicken over the heat for another minute, then spoon the chicken and sauce into a shallow serving dish and cover loosely with foil. The chicken may now be kept warm for up to an hour without spoiling in the lowest possible oven.

TO SERVE Just before serving, strew the dish with rocket leaves. This dish goes particularly well with new potatoes and a green vegetable, or with egg noodles or tagliatelle.

Serves 6

PUMPKIN STUFFED WITH SPICED TURKEY AND CASHEW NUTS

If you want an impressive centrepiece for a Hallowe'en supper, this is ideal.

> *375g (12oz) skinless turkey breast*
> *   fillets*
> *4 tablespoons olive oil*
> *25g (1oz) butter*
> *1 large onion, chopped finely*
> *1 teaspoon ground mace*
> *1 teaspoon paprika*
> *1 teaspoon dill seeds*
> *3 large garlic cloves, chopped finely*
> *2.5–5cm (1–2-inch) piece of fresh*
> *   root ginger, chopped finely*
> *125g (4oz) unroasted cashew nuts*
> *250g (8oz) turkey or chicken livers*
> *6–8 sage leaves, sliced thinly*
> *1.5kg (3½lb) pumpkin, large squash*
> *   or marrow*
> *Sea salt*
> *Black pepper*

Set the oven to preheat at Gas Mark 4/180°C/350°F. Cut the turkey breasts into small pieces. Put two tablespoons of the olive oil and all the butter in a large sauté pan over a medium heat. Add the onion to the sauté pan and stir until soft; then stir in the mace, the paprika and dill seeds, followed by the finely chopped garlic and ginger. Add the turkey pieces to the sauté pan and stir until the meat is opaque. Turn this mixture into a bowl. Add a further tablespoon of oil to the pan. Add the cashew nuts and stir around briskly over an increased heat until they have turned brown, then add the nuts to the spiced turkey mixture in the bowl. Finally, slice the turkey livers. Place the remaining oil in the pan and sauté the livers briefly. Add the livers and the sage leaves to the turkey mixture.

Season generously with sea salt and black pepper.

Now cut the top off the pumpkin, or if you are using a marrow, halve it lengthways. Scrape out all the seeds and strands with a metal spoon. Pack the stuffing into the cavity. Replace the top and wrap the pumpkin in foil. Bake in a roasting tin for two hours or until the flesh feels soft when you insert a small long knife.

TO SERVE Unwrap the pumpkin and put it on a serving plate. If you have used a pumpkin or a round squash which stands upright, take off the top and scoop out both pumpkin flesh and filling together on to individual plates. Cut a marrow across in thick slices. Accompany with some buttered noodles and a simple green salad.
Serves 4

TURKEY AND CUCUMBER STRIPS IN SPRING ONION AND ANCHOVY SAUCE

A quick, low-fat supper: the turkey and cucumber are poached in a stock with Chinese aromatics, which then forms the base of the spring onion and anchovy sauce.

> *50g (2oz) can of anchovy fillets*
> *1 chicken stock cube*
> *900ml (1½ pints) hot water*
> *2 large garlic cloves, chopped*
> *   roughly*
> *5cm (2-inch) piece of fresh root*
> *   ginger, chopped roughly*
> *5–8cm (2–3-inch) stick of*
> *   cinnamon, broken in half*
> *2 star anise*
> *1 small cucumber, peeled, halved*
> *   and sliced thinly lengthways*
> *500g (1lb) skinless turkey breast*
> *   fillets, sliced thinly*
> *1 tablespoon cornflour*
> *1 tablespoon soy sauce*
> *   (approximately)*
> *2–4 pinches of chilli powder*
> *1 bunch of spring onions, sliced*
> *   across in 1cm (½-inch) pieces*

◀ *Pumpkin stuffed with spiced turkey and cashew nuts*

Empty the anchovies and their oil into a heatproof bowl set over a pan of gently simmering water. Stir constantly for a few minutes until the anchovies have dissolved. Remove from the heat.

Put the stock cube and hot water into a large saucepan. Place the garlic, ginger, cinnamon and star anise on a piece of muslin and tie up the top securely to form a little bag. Add the bag to the stock in the pan and stir gently to dissolve the stock cube. Bring to the boil and simmer for about five minutes. Add the cucumber and simmer for three minutes. Lift out the cucumber with a slotted spoon and remove any excess moisture with kitchen paper. Put the cucumber on to a large warmed serving dish. Bring the stock to the boil again, add the turkey slices and simmer very gently for a further 3–5 minutes, just until they turn opaque. Add them to the cucumber.

Dissolve the cornflour in a little water in a cup and stir into the stock. Bring the stock to the boil and bubble, stirring, for three minutes. Then add the reserved anchovy mixture and soy sauce. Add 2–4 pinches of chilli

powder to taste. Remove the bag and strain the sauce into a clean pan. Bring the sauce just up to the boil again, stir in the spring onions for 30 seconds and then pour the sauce over the turkey and cucumber and serve at once.
Serves 4

▲ *Turkey and cucumber strips in spring onion and anchovy sauce*

VIETNAMESE CHICKEN NOODLE HOTPOT WITH FRESH LEAVES

I developed this to remind myself of some of the wonderful hotpots and soups I had while travelling in Vietnam.

125g (4oz) thin wheat noodles
2 fresh red chillies
3 chicken breasts
1.2 litres (2 pints) chicken stock
50g (2oz) coconut milk powder or
*   125g (4oz) creamed coconut*
4 tablespoons lemon juice
Mixture of salad leaves, including
*   plenty of fresh mint*
2 tablespoons groundnut oil
5cm (2-inch) piece of fresh root
*   ginger, finely chopped*
3 large garlic cloves, chopped finely
3–4 Thai lime leaves (optional)
250g (8oz) beansprouts
125g (4oz) peeled prawns
Generous handful of fresh coriander
Salt

Boil the noodles in salted water until they are just soft. Drain the noodles through a strainer, then run through with cold water to halt the cooking process. Leave the noodles on one side.

Cut the chillies in half under running water, discard the seeds and stem and cut very finely into strips. Remove any skin or bone from the chicken breasts, then slice them across fairly thinly. In a saucepan, heat the chicken stock to boiling point, add the coconut milk powder or cream and stir until the coconut has dissolved. Then add the lemon juice to the saucepan.

Before cooking, mix up the salad leaves and mint and put them into a serving bowl or into four individual bowls. Heat the groundnut oil over a medium heat in a wok or large saucepan, add the chopped ginger and garlic and the sliced chicken and stir for about two minutes. Then finely chop the Thai lime leaves (if you have been able to get them), and add them together with the sliced chillies and the bean sprouts. Stir for 1–2 minutes until the bean sprouts are limp. Now pour in the chicken stock and coconut milk mixture and finally stir in the cooked noodles. Bring the mixture up to bubbling, remove the pan from the heat and add the peeled prawns. Taste and add salt if you think it necessary. Finally, roughly chop the coriander leaves and add them to the soup.
TO SERVE Transfer to a heated soup tureen. Following the wonderfully refreshing Vietnamese custom, place a large bowl of fresh leaves, including plenty of mint, on the table, for guests to throw handfuls of the leaves into their food as it is served.
Serves 4

QUAILS WITH TOMATO, ANCHOVY AND FRESH MINT SAUCE

These tiny birds are best cooked slowly so the flesh is easy to cut from the bone.

375g (12oz) ripe tomatoes
2 small garlic cloves, chopped finely
½ tablespoon tomato purée
2½ tablespoons fresh orange juice
15g (½oz) butter
8 bay leaves
8 quails
3 anchovy fillets and their oil
150ml (¼ pint) double cream
Handful of fresh mint leaves,
*   chopped finely*
Olive oil, for brushing
Salt and black pepper

Set the oven to preheat at Gas Mark 3/160°C/325°F. In a bowl, cover the tomatoes with boiling water for 2–3 minutes; then drain and skin them and chop the flesh very finely. Put the chopped tomatoes and garlic into a bowl, add the tomato purée, orange juice, and a sprinkling of salt and black pepper and mix thoroughly. Butter the base of a large roasting tin, then spread the tomato mixture evenly in the tin. Put a bay leaf into the body cavity of each quail and arrange the birds closely together on top of the tomato mixture. Brush the breast of each quail with olive oil and sprinkle with a little salt. Cover tightly with buttered foil and cook in the centre of the oven for 1¼ hours. Then remove the foil and put the tin back in the oven for a further 30 minutes. During this time, place the anchovy fillets and their oil in a small heatproof bowl set over a pan of gently simmering water. Stir over the heat until the anchovies dissolve to a creamy consistency and leave on one side.

When the quails are ready, use a wide, slotted spatula to transfer them to a large, warm serving dish, tipping any juices from their body cavity back into the roasting tin as you do so. Put the tin over the heat on top of the stove, stir the dissolved anchovy mixture into the tomato mixture and juices and bring up to bubbling point. Then stir in the cream and allow the mixture to bubble, stirring for 3–5 minutes, to thicken it slightly. Stir in the mint and pour the sauce into a sauce jug to serve immediately with the quails.
Serves 4

▲ *Quails with tomato, anchovy and fresh mint sauce*

◄ *Vietnamese chicken noodle hotpot with fresh leaves*

GUINEA FOWL WITH LAST-LICK SAUCE

My son found the anchovy and rosemary sauce in this dish so irresistible that he used his finger to lick up every last speck of it!

1.1kg (2½lb) leeks, sliced
1.1kg (2½lb) small potatoes, peeled and sliced thinly
2 small branches fresh bay leaves
5–6 tablespoons extra virgin olive oil
3 tablespoons sherry vinegar
2 guinea fowl
4–5 garlic cloves
300ml (½ pint) double cream
300ml (½ pint) milk
50g (2oz) can of anchovies
Generous sprig of fresh rosemary
6 sun-dried tomatoes
Salt and black pepper

Set the oven to preheat at Gas Mark 6/200°C/400°F. Put the slices of leek on the bottom of a large, deep roasting pan. Arrange the potato slices among the leeks, sprinkle with salt and pepper and lay the bay leaf branches between them in a central layer. Dribble the olive oil and sherry vinegar over the top, then lay the guinea fowl on the potatoes and leeks. Smear the birds with a little more olive oil and sprinkle with salt and pepper. Cover the roasting pan with two layers of foil, folded and pressed around the edges to keep the moisture in.

Cook the birds on the centre shelf of the oven for 1¾ hours, taking the foil off for the last 15 minutes. While the guinea fowl are cooking, put the garlic in a small saucepan with the cream and milk. Stir together, then add the whole anchovy fillets to the mixture together with the rosemary and a sprinkling of salt and pepper. Put the pan over the heat, bring the mixture just up to the boil, then lower the heat and simmer as gently as possible for 25–35 minutes, stirring often, until the garlic cloves are soft and the creamy mixture is the thickness of a pouring sauce. While the sauce is simmering, slice the sun-dried tomatoes very thinly.

When the sauce has cooked, strain it into another saucepan, pressing the garlic and anchovies through with a wooden spoon. Stir the mixture together and then keep on one side.

Just before you are ready to eat, reheat the sauce gently, adding the sun-dried tomatoes. Pour the sauce into a serving jug. Remove the guinea fowl from the oven and put them on to a carving board. Take out the leeks and potatoes with a slotted spatula and put them together in a serving bowl. Boil up the juices in the roasting pan over a high heat for 2–3 minutes, or until the juices have reduced quite a bit, then pour them over the vegetables.

TO SERVE Carve into neat slices and serve on individual plates with a little cream sauce poured over, and accompanied by the vegetables.
Serves 6

SAUTÉED DUCK BREASTS ON A BED OF RED PEPPER AND SPINACH

If possible, use Barbary duck with its lovely gamey flavour for this dish.

2 large duck breasts fillets (625–750g/1¼–1½lb total weight)
2 teaspoon coriander seeds
1 teaspoon black peppercorns
2 large garlic cloves, chopped finely
1 rounded teaspoon dried oregano
7 tablespoons olive oil
4 tablespoons lemon juice
3 large red peppers
1 large onion, chopped
3 pinches of chilli powder
1 dessertspoon caster sugar
250g (8oz) small leaf spinach
2 tablespoons pumpkin seeds (optional)
Generous handful of lovage leaves or flat leaf parsley, chopped
Sea salt

◄ *Guinea fowl with last-lick sauce; sautéed duck breasts on a bed of red pepper and spinach*

Remove and discard the skin of the duck fillets. Then slice the meat across in 3mm (⅛-inch) slices and put into a bowl. Put the coriander seeds and black peppercorns into a pestle and mortar and grind them together, but not too finely. Add the garlic, coriander and black peppercorns to the sliced duck in the bowl with the oregano, two tablespoons of the olive oil and the lemon juice. Stir thoroughly, cover the bowl and leave on one side at room temperature.

Slice the peppers in half, discard the seeds and stem and cut the peppers up roughly into 1cm (½-inch) pieces. Place 4 tablespoons of the olive oil into a large, heavy-based sauté pan over a low to medium heat. Add the peppers and onions and cook for 15–20 minutes, stirring now and then until both pepper and onion are really soft. Then add the chilli powder and the sugar and a good sprinkling of salt. Stir the mixture well and remove the pan from the heat. Bring a saucepan of water to the boil, throw in the spinach leaves for just 30 seconds until they are wilted; then drain the leaves well, pressing out any excess liquid with the back of a spoon. Stir the wilted leaves into the pepper mixture and turn the mixture into a warmed, large shallow dish. Put the dish into a very low oven to keep warm while you cook the duck.

Put the remaining tablespoon of olive oil in a wok or wide, heavy frying pan or casserole over a high heat. When the oil is smoking add the marinated duck slices and the pumpkin seeds if using. Flash-fry the duck for 20–30 seconds until it is cooked but still pink-fleshed. Finally, stir in the lovage leaves or parsley. Spoon the duck on to the pepper mixture, piling it up, and serve at once.

TO SERVE I usually serve this with egg tagliatelle or boiled new potatoes, and french beans.
Serves 4

STEAMED CHICKEN BALLS WITH CORIANDER LEAF MAYONNAISE

These chicken balls and their fragrant mayonnaise are good for a cold meal.

FOR THE CHICKEN BALLS:
  375g (12oz) skinless chicken breast
    fillets
  1 fresh red chilli
  2.5cm (1-inch) piece of root ginger
  6–8 spring onions, chopped finely
  50g (2oz) fresh white breadcrumbs
  Finely grated zest of 1 lemon
  1 large egg white (size 1)
  Salt
FOR THE MAYONNAISE:
  1 egg (size 1), at room temperature
  1 egg yolk (size 1)
  1 garlic clove, crushed
  2 tablespoons lemon juice
  Generous handful of fresh coriander
  300ml (½ pint) extra virgin olive oil
    (approximately)
  Salt and black pepper

To make the chicken balls, roughly cut up the chicken breast and place the pieces in a food processor. Whizz the chicken until finely chopped and turn it into a mixing bowl. Cut the chilli open under running water, discard the seeds and stem and then cut the flesh across into the thinnest possible strips. Peel and finely chop the ginger. Add the chilli, ginger and spring onions to the chicken together with the breadcrumbs, lemon zest, egg white and a liberal sprinkling of salt. Using a wooden spoon, stir very thoroughly. Then, using wet hands, roll and form this mixture into small balls about the size of a walnut. Put the balls in a steaming tray over gently boiling water, cover and steam for 8–10 minutes or until they are cooked right through. Leave until cold.

To make the mayonnaise, put the egg and egg yolk in a food processor with the crushed garlic and lemon juice. Whizz together, and while still whizzing, begin adding the oil in a thin stream, gradually at first. When you have a fairly thick coating consistency, roughly chop the coriander leaves, but reserve several sprigs for garnish. Whizz the chopped coriander leaves into the mayonnaise until well blended. Season the mayonnaise with salt and black pepper. Turn the mayonnaise into a mixing bowl, cover it with clingfilm and put in the refrigerator. Before serving, add the cooked chicken balls to the mayonnaise and, using a wooden spoon, mix together gently to coat the chicken balls thoroughly.

TO SERVE Spoon the mixture on to a pretty serving dish and garnish with the reserved sprigs of coriander leaves.

Serves 4

STUFFED AND ROLLED CHICKEN FILLETS WITH ORANGE AND MUSHROOM SAUCE

If you prefer, you can substitute lemon for orange in this lovely dish. To pound out chicken fillets, space them out on a sheet of oiled greaseproof paper, place another oiled sheet over the top and pound them with a rolling pin or mallet.

  2 medium chicory, chopped finely
  Finely grated zest and juice of
    1 orange
  50g (2oz) can of anchovy fillets
  3 garlic cloves
  2.5cm (1-inch) piece of fresh root
    ginger, chopped finely
  2–3 pinches of chilli powder
  4 skinless chicken breast fillets,
    pounded out as thinly as possible
  Caster sugar, to sprinkle
  2 tablespoons olive oil
  300ml (½ pint) milk
  2 rounded teaspoons arrowroot or
    cornflour
  50g (2oz) mushrooms, sliced thinly
  Generous handful of flat leaf
    parsley, chopped roughly

◄ *Steamed chicken balls with coriander leaf mayonnaise*

Set the oven to preheat at Gas Mark 4/180°C/350°F. To make the stuffing, put the chopped chicory into a bowl with the orange zest. Drain the oil from the anchovies into the bowl, then finely chop the anchovy fillets and add them to the stuffing mixture. Add the garlic and the ginger, then the chilli powder and mix together thoroughly.

Pat the stuffing evenly and firmly all over the pounded chicken fillets. Roll the fillets up gently and place them in an ovenproof gratin dish, join side down. Sprinkle them lightly with caster sugar and smear them with a little olive oil. Pour the orange juice into the dish around the rolls. Cover with foil and cook in the centre of the oven for 40–45 minutes. Remove the chicken rolls carefully on to a serving dish and keep warm in a low oven, covered.

Strain the juices from the chicken into a saucepan and add the milk. Mix the arrowroot or cornflour with a very little water and then stir this into the juice mixture. Put the pan over the heat and bring the mixture to the boil, stirring all the time. Allow the mixture to bubble, still stirring, for two minutes until it is thickened and smooth. Add the sliced mushrooms and bubble for another minute. Finally, still stirring, add the chopped parsley. Spoon the sauce over the rolls just before serving.

Serves 4

▲ *Stuffed and rolled chicken fillets with orange and mushroom sauce*

CORN-FED CHICKEN WITH CURRIED FENNEL SAUCE

In this dish the chicken is cooked in a pot with spices, yogurt and fennel.

  1 tablespoon groundnut oil
  15g (1oz) butter
  4 corn-fed chicken joints
    (1.5kg/3½lb)
  2 large fennel bulbs
  3 cardamom pods
  2 large garlic cloves
  2.5cm (1-inch) piece of root ginger
  1 fresh red chilli
  1 teaspoon ground coriander
  ½ teaspoon ground cinnamon
  ¼ teaspoon ground cloves
  1 tablespoon plain flour
  150ml (¼ pint) natural yogurt
  8 tablespoons lemon juice
  1½ tablespoons tomato purée mixed
    into 300ml (½ pint) water
  Generous handful of fresh coriander
    leaves, chopped roughly
  Salt

Set the oven to preheat at Gas Mark 6/200°C/400°F. Heat the oil and half the butter in a large frying pan over a high heat. Add the chicken pieces and brown them all over. Put the chicken into a large casserole. Leave the unwashed frying pan to one side. Cut off the base and stalks of the fennel, remove any marked outer parts and cut the bulbs into 6–8 pieces each. Put the fennel in the dish around the chicken. Roughly crush the cardamom pods and scatter them in with the fennel. Peel the garlic and ginger and chop finely. Cut the chilli open lengthways under running water, discard the seeds and stem and then slice across very thinly.

Put the frying pan back over a gentle heat, adding the remaining butter. Add the garlic, ginger, chilli and the ground spices, and stir for 30 seconds. Then stir in the flour and continue stirring over the heat for about one minute or until smooth. Stir in the yogurt in one direction only. Add the lemon juice to the tomato purée and water mixture. Then very gradually stir the tomato purée mixture into the fried spices. Stirring all the time, increase the heat and bring the mixture to boiling point. Stir until the sauce thickens, and season it to taste with a little salt. Pour the sauce over the fennel in the casserole dish.

Cover the dish and place in the centre of the preheated oven. After one hour, reduce the heat to Gas Mark 3/160°C/325°F and cook for a further 30 minutes.
TO SERVE Remove the chicken pieces from the casserole with a slotted spoon and fork and put onto a serving plate. Add the coriander leaves to the fennel sauce and serve separately. Serve with basmati rice and a green vegetable.
Serves 4

GLAZED GUINEA FOWL WITH BLUEBERRY AND SHALLOT SAUCE

Guinea fowl are very lean birds with a fine texture and delicate, gamey flavour. The sauce accompanying these glossy brown birds is equally dark and shiny with a lovely sweet and sour flavour.

  2 guinea fowl
  150–175g (5–6oz) thinly sliced
    streaky unsmoked bacon
    (optional)
  FOR THE SAUCE:
    250g (8oz) shallots, halved
      lengthways
    1 small sprig of fresh rosemary,
      chopped finely
    250g (8oz) fresh blueberries
    450ml (¾ pint) freshly squeezed
      orange juice
    50g (2oz) caster sugar
    2 tablespoons sherry vinegar
    1 tablespoon water
    1 dessertspoon cornflour
    Salt
    Black pepper

◄ *Corn-fed chicken with curried fennel sauce*

Set the oven to preheat at Gas Mark 4/180°C/350°F. Put the birds into a roasting pan and either brush the breasts with olive oil or lay the strips of bacon (if using) lengthways all over the breast. Roast in the centre of the oven for 1½ hours. Then remove the bacon, sprinkle the birds evenly with a little salt and caster sugar and put them back on a high shelf of the oven for 15–20 minutes or until the birds turn a glossy, dark brown. Turn off the heat and leave them in the oven with the door open while you prepare the sauce.

To make the sauce, put the shallots, rosemary and blueberries into a saucepan with the orange juice and the sugar. Bring the mixture to the boil, then simmer gently, uncovered, stirring often, for about 25 minutes or until the shallots and blueberries are completely soft. Remove from the heat. Put the vinegar and the water into a cup. Add the cornflour, stir until smooth and then stir into the blueberry mixture with a wooden spoon. Put the pan back on the heat and bring to the boil, stirring until the sauce thickens. Season to taste with salt and plenty of black pepper.
TO SERVE Carve the birds and serve with the sauce and a green vegetable.
Serves 6–8

▲ *Glazed guinea fowl with blueberry and shallot sauce*

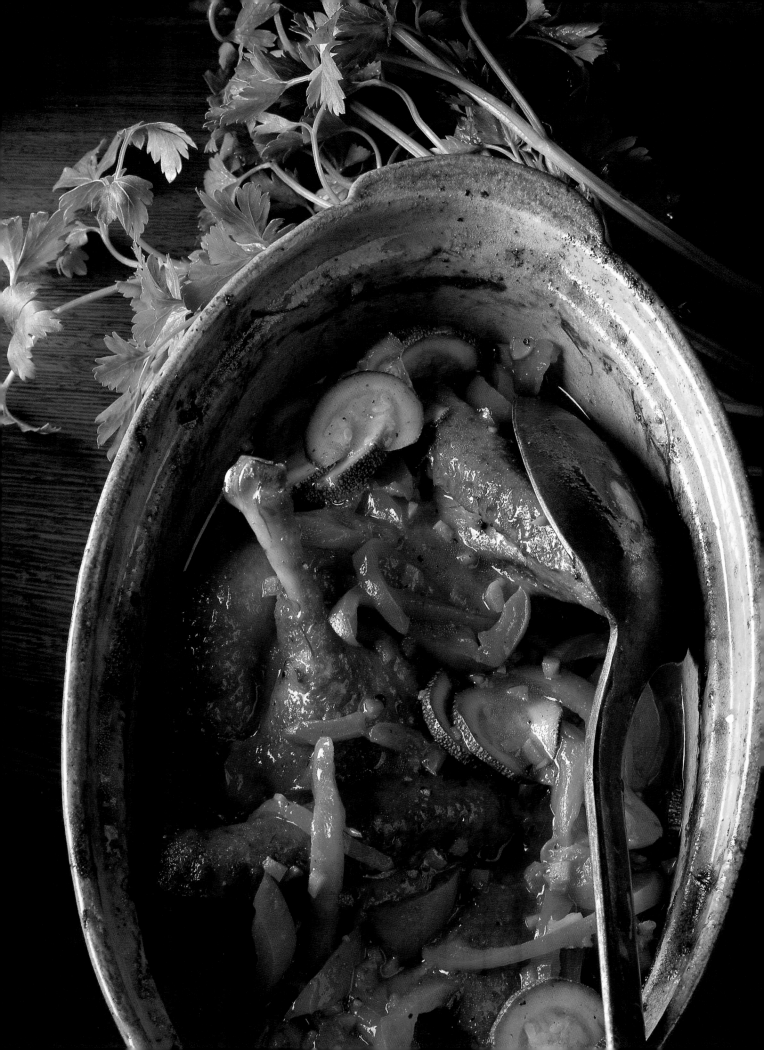

JOINTS OF DUCK WITH SAFFRON, RED PEPPERS AND COURGETTES

You can make this glowing casserole ahead of time and keep it warm, adding the courgettes at the last moment.

Generous pinch of saffron strands
2 large red peppers
5cm (2-inch) piece of root ginger
4 large garlic cloves
25g (1oz) butter
2 tablespoons olive oil
6 duck joints
3 teaspoons paprika
40g (1½oz) plain flour
300ml (½ pint) strained, freshly
  squeezed orange juice
4 tablespoons lemon juice
3–4 pinches of chilli powder
500g (1lb) courgettes
Salt

Put the saffron strands into a measuring jug and add 150ml (¼ pint) of boiling water. Leave it to infuse. Cut open the peppers, discard the seeds and stem and slice the flesh across very thinly. Chop the ginger and the garlic.

Melt the butter with the olive oil in a large casserole over a medium heat. Add the duck joints and fry on both sides just until the skin has browned and fat is running out. Remove all but a tablespoonful of fat. Then stir in the paprika, followed by the chopped ginger and garlic. Set the oven to preheat at Gas Mark 3/160°C/325°F.

Remove the casserole from the heat and stir in the flour, followed by the sliced peppers, the saffron water and the strained orange and lemon juice.

Stir well, season with salt and chilli powder to taste. Then put the casserole back over the heat and bring the mixture to the boil. Stir continually until the juices have thickened.

Finally, cover the casserole and put it in the centre of the oven for 1–1¼ hours. Cut the courgettes across in half and then slice the halves very thinly lengthways. Bring a saucepan of salted water to the boil, add the courgette slices and cook for two minutes or until just softened. Drain the courgettes and add them to the casserole dish.
TO SERVE Serve immediately with waxy new potatoes and a lettuce salad, which is excellent when wilted under the hot juices of the casserole.
Serves 6

INDIAN SPICED AND FRUITED DUCK BREAST SLICES IN MUSHROOM PURÉE

If they are available, use Barbary duck breast fillets as they have a slightly more gamey flavour. Also, it is well worth buying the fresh spices and grinding them yourself in a coffee grinder or a mortar and pestle – their aroma is incomparable. This dish is excellent for entertaining as it can be prepared well in advance.

4 duck breast fillets, approx 1.15kg
  (2¾lb) total weight
6 cloves
10 cardamom pods
1½ teaspoons coriander seeds
3 blades mace, or 1 teaspoon
  ground mace
1 fresh red or green chilli
1 small red pepper
250g (8oz) mushrooms
150ml (¼ pint) chicken stock
2.5cm (1-inch) piece of fresh root
  ginger, chopped finely
3 garlic cloves, chopped finely
175g (6oz) seedless grapes
500g (1lb) spinach, chopped
  roughly
Salt
Coriander leaves, to garnish

◄ *Joints of duck with saffron, red peppers and courgettes*

Prick the skin of the duck fillets all over with a fork. Heat a large, dry frying pan over a medium heat. Put the duck, skin side down, into the pan and fry just until the skin is golden brown and quite a lot of fat has run out. Using a slotted spatula, transfer the duck from the pan to a chopping board. Reserve the fat in the pan.

Now grind the cloves, cardamom, coriander seeds and mace. Cut the chilli open under running water, remove the seeds and stem and slice across very thinly. Halve the pepper lengthways, remove the seeds and stem and slice the flesh across. Purée the mushrooms in a processor. Lastly, cut the duck across in 1cm (½-inch) slices.

Put two tablespoons of the duck fat in a large casserole over a medium heat. Add the ground spices through a sieve and stir for just 30 seconds. Add the garlic and ginger and stir for another 30 seconds. Add the mushroom purée, the chilli and red pepper, stir once and remove from the heat. Stir in the stock and add the sliced duck.

Bring the casserole up to bubbling, cover, and braise the duck gently for about 45–60 minutes or until the duck is tender, adding the grapes ten minutes

before the end. Once the duck is cooked, you can remove it from the heat and keep it warm, covered, in a very low oven.

To finish the cooking, put the casserole back over a fairly high heat on top of the stove. Season to taste with salt, if necessary, and stir in the spinach leaves. Bubble the juices for a couple of minutes to cook the spinach.
TO SERVE Garnish the dish with the coriander and serve with basmati rice.
Serves 6–8

▲ *Indian spiced and fruited duck breast slices in mushroom purée*

EXOTIC CHICKEN PIE

This pie might have been put together by an Anglo-Indian cook during the British Raj in India.

FOR THE PASTRY:
  275g (9oz) strong plain flour
  25g (1oz) ground rice
  ½ teaspoon salt
  2 teaspoons ground turmeric
  1 teaspoon ground coriander
  175g (6oz) cold butter, cut into
    small pieces
  2 tablespoons very cold water
    (approximately)
FOR THE FILLING:
  1 onion, roughly chopped
  1 carrot, scraped and chopped
  3–4 cardamom pods
  50g (2oz) butter
  2 teaspoons ground cinnamon
  2 rounded teaspoons mustard seeds
  4 tablespoons lemon juice
  250ml (8 fl oz) water
  2 fresh red chillies
  250g (8oz) curd cheese
  3 large garlic cloves, chopped
  2.5cm (1-inch) piece of fresh root
    ginger, chopped
  875g (1¾lb) skinless chicken
    breasts, sliced thinly
  175g (6oz) chestnut mushrooms,
    sliced thinly
  Sea salt

To make the pastry, put the flour, ground rice, salt, turmeric and coriander into a bowl. Mix the ingredients together. Add the butter pieces to the flour mixture and rub the mixture with your finger tips until it resembles rough bread crumbs. Add just enough of the very cold water, stirring with a knife, until the pastry just begins to stick together. Gather up the dough into a ball. Wrap the dough in clingfilm and put it to chill in the refrigerator. Then make the filling. Put the chopped onion and carrot into a food processor and whizz until the mixture is as fine as possible. Remove the cardamom seeds from their pods and grind them with a pestle and mortar. Melt the butter in a casserole dish on top of the stove over a medium heat. Then add the ground cardamom seeds, cinnamon and the mustard seeds and stir for 30 seconds. Next add the puréed onion and carrot, and stir for a few minutes. Then add the lemon juice and water. Cover the casserole and put it over a very gentle heat for about 30 minutes. The sauce should be the consistency of thick cream.

Meanwhile, cut the chillies open lengthways under running water, discard the seeds and stem and slice the flesh across finely. When the onion and carrot mixture is well cooked and mushy, add the curd cheese. Stir until the curd cheese has melted, then add the prepared garlic, ginger and chilli and sliced chicken and mushrooms. Sprinkle the mixture with a little sea salt and stir together. Bring the mixture up to bubbling again on top of the stove. Cover the casserole, lower the heat and simmer the chicken very gently indeed for 30 minutes, stirring occasionally. Then remove the casserole from the heat, and add a little more salt, to taste, if necessary. Spoon the mixture into a pie dish and leave the mixture to cool. When it is quite cold, set the oven to preheat at Gas Mark 6/200°C/400°F. Take the pastry from the refrigerator and roll it out on a floured surface into a size big enough to cover the pie dish. Moisten the edges of the dish and lay the pastry on top. Press the edges down lightly and trim neatly with a knife. Press the trimmings together, roll the remaining pastry out and cut out decorations for the top of the pie. Piece two small holes in the pastry to allow the steam to escape. Cook the pie on the centre shelf of the oven for 25–30 minutes.
TO SERVE Serve hot with a mixed green salad or a green vegetable.
Serves 6

ROAST CHICKEN WITH COURGETTE AND CRANBERRY SAUCE

Cranberries and courgettes are an interesting contrast in this low-fat sauce.

  1 lemon
  1.5–1.75kg (3½–4lb) fresh chicken
  Olive oil, to smear
FOR THE SAUCE:
  4 large garlic cloves, chopped
  175ml (6 fl oz) chicken stock
  1 rounded teaspoon dried oregano
  250g (8oz) courgettes, chopped
  750g (1½lb) cranberries
  Handful of parsley, chopped
  Salt and black pepper

◄ *Exotic chicken pie; roast chicken with courgette and cranberry sauce*

Heat the oven to gas 6/200°C/400°F. Squeeze the lemon juice into a saucepan. Put the lemon skin in the body cavity of the chicken. Sprinkle the chicken with salt and pepper and smear with olive oil. Then roast in the centre of the oven for 1–1¼ hours.

Meanwhile, prepare the sauce. Add the garlic to the lemon juice in the saucepan. Add the chicken stock to the saucepan with the oregano. Bring to the boil, cover the pan and simmer gently for about 10 minutes until the garlic is soft. Add the courgettes, cover the pan again and simmer for a few minutes until the courgettes are just soft. Place the contents of the pan into a food processor and whizz until smooth. Put the courgette purée back in the pan and add the cranberries. Cover the pan and simmer again for about five minutes until the cranberries are just soft and beginning to pop out of their skins. Remove the pan from the heat and leave on one side.

When the chicken is cooked, pour the juices from the body cavity and any in the roasting tin into the sauce into the saucepan, pouring off excess fat. Put the sauce back on the heat to reheat. Lastly, stir in the chopped parsley and pour the sauce into a bowl to serve with the chicken.
Serves 5–6

VEGETABLE MAIN DISHES

This chapter was my greatest challenge. I love cooking vegetables; their variety of colour, shape and texture offers constant inspiration. Yet creating a main dish consisting entirely of vegetables, which is sustaining enough without being stodgy, is not easy. I am sure many people have memories of shapeless vegetarian dishes, always brown, and either mushy, or with so much fibre that they leave you feeling completely bloated. However, vegetarian food has changed a lot over the last years and a good principal dish can be more exciting than when meat, fish or poultry is the main ingredient. Increasingly, different vegetables are available to us and flavourings are wide-ranging and often subtle or unique. Since I am not a vegetarian myself, I found I had far more ideas if I was cooking for someone who was. Therefore my oldest daughter and a few vegetarian friends have been extremely useful when working on the recipes for this chapter. A vegetarian main dish should not be simply a larger version of an accompanying dish but something which makes as much of an impact as a meat-based dish. You should think of it as the star turn of the meal; it must arrest the attention and remain in the memory both for its appearance and its taste. Many of the dishes in the pasta, rice and pulses chapter also have these qualities.

PEPPERS FILLED WITH GARLIC POTATOES
AND COOKED IN OLIVE OIL

You can make this simple vegetarian dish with red, yellow or green peppers or with a mixture of all three. The combination of the sweetness of the peppers and garlicky potatoes is quite delicious and dill seeds and potatoes seem to have one of those magical affinities, that cannot be bettered.

8 large peppers
750g (1½lb) large salad potatoes
6 large garlic cloves, chopped finely
2 teaspoons dill seeds
175ml (6 fl oz) olive oil
Sea salt
Black pepper

◀ *Peppers filled with garlic potatoes and cooked in olive oil*

Set the oven to preheat at Gas Mark 4/180°C/350°F. Cut just the stem part off the top of the peppers and, using your fingers, remove all the seeds and inner core. Scrub the potatoes and cut them into very small cubes. Put the cubed potatoes in a bowl and stir in the chopped garlic, the dill seeds and three tablespoons of the olive oil. Season the mixture well with sea salt and plenty of black pepper. Spoon this potato mixture into the hollowed out peppers, pressing the stuffing in firmly. Arrange the filled peppers in a large casserole dish, placing the open ends against the sides of the dish to help keep in the potatoes. Pour the remaining olive oil all over the peppers and cover the casserole dish.

Put the casserole on the centre shelf of the preheated oven for 1½ hours. Remove the dish from the oven and, using a slotted spatula, carefully lift out the peppers and place them on a large flat, heated serving plate. Place the casserole on top of the stove and bring the pepper juices to the boil. Alternatively, place the juices in a saucepan. Bubble the juices fiercely for 2–5 minutes until they are reduced and thickened. Just before serving, pour the reduced juices over the peppers .
TO SERVE This can be served hot or cold. The pepper juices are delicious soaked up and eaten with crusty bread.A lightly steamed green vegetable is also good.
Serves 4

LEEK AND AUBERGINE CHARLOTTE WITH SUN-DRIED TOMATOES

A golden, crisp bread crust encases a luscious filling of leeks and aubergines.

2 tablespoons wine vinegar
375–425g (12–14oz) aubergine
750g (1½lb) trimmed leeks
300ml (½ pint) olive oil
  (approximately)
½ teaspoon green peppercorns
8 sun-dried tomatoes, sliced thinly
1 large square white loaf, sliced
  thinly
Salt and black pepper

Half-fill a saucepan with salted water, add the wine vinegar and bring to the boil. Cut the aubergine into rounds and then into cubes, adding them to the boiling water immediately they are cut. Stir the cubes, then cover and boil briskly for two minutes. Drain and pat off excess moisture with kitchen paper.

Cut the leeks across in 1cm (½-inch) slices. Put four tablespoons of the olive oil in a large, heavy saucepan over a medium heat. Add the leeks, aubergine cubes and green peppercorns. Stir the mixture, then cover and cook for 10–15 minutes until the leeks are soft. Uncover, and stir for 1–2 minutes until all the liquid is evaporated. Remove the pan from the heat. Stir in the sun-dried tomatoes, and season generously.

Set the oven to preheat at Gas Mark 5/190°C/375°F .Oil a 1.5-litre (2½-pint) charlotte mould or cake tin. Pour the remaining olive oil ·into a shallow dish. Cut the crust off a slice of bread and dip the bread into the oil in the dish so that it is thoroughly smeared with oil on both sides. Lay the oiled bread in the bottom of the mould. Line the base with with bread slices in this way, and continue up the sides,

overlapping the slices and bringing them up over the rim by about 2.5cm (1 inch). You may need a little more oil to complete this process. Then spoon the leek and aubergine mixture into the lined mould, packing it well down. Turn the overlapping edges of the bread in over the top of the filling. Finally place a further slice of oiled bread in the centre so that the filling is completely enclosed. Place a metal plate or sandwich tin on top so that the bread edges won't curl up, but the air must be able to get in around the edges so that the charlotte doesn't steam. Cook in the centre of the oven for one hour. Turn out on to an ovenproof serving plate. Put the tin or plate back on top and place the charlotte back in the oven for 10–15 minutes until it is golden brown and crisp all over.
Serves 4–5

ROOT VEGETABLE PIE WITH PARSNIP PASTRY

I have a particular fondness for root vegetables; during the chilly grey days of winter, I find their sweet earthy flavours very soothing.

FOR THE PASTRY:
  375g (12oz) parsnips, chopped
  300g (10oz) plain flour
  2 teaspoons baking powder
  1 teaspoon salt
  175g (6oz) butter, cut into dice
  1 egg yolk
FOR THE FILLING:
  250g (8oz) frozen sweetcorn
  375g (12oz) small carrots
  250g (8oz) turnips
  75g (3oz) butter
  3 onions, sliced in rings
  1 teaspoon ground coriander
  1 rounded teaspoon caraway seeds
  2 teaspoons coarse grain mustard
  1 rounded tablespoon plain flour
  300ml (½ pint) cider
  150ml (¼ pint) soured cream
  Salt and black pepper

◄ *Leek and aubergine charlotte with sun-dried tomatoes*

To make the pastry, boil the parsnips until soft. Mash them thoroughly and leave to cool. Then sift the flour and baking powder into a bowl and season well. Rub the butter into the flour with your fingertips until it resembles breadcrumbs. Stir in the cold mashed parsnips until smooth. Wrap in clingfilm and refrigerate.

Blanch the sweetcorn, drain and set to one side. Slice the carrots and turnips thinly, boil in salted water until soft, and then drain. Melt the butter in a large heavy pan over a medium heat. Add the onions and stir until soft. Stir in the coriander and the caraway seeds and remove from the heat. Then stir in the mustard and flour until smooth. Stir in the cider and return the pan to the heat. Bring to the boil, stirring, until the mixture thickens. Continue stirring for two minutes, then add the sweetcorn. Remove from the heat. Stir in the carrots, turnips and cream. Season to taste, turn the mixture into a pie dish and leave to cool.

Using a floured rolling pin, roll out the pastry on a lightly floured surface.

Place the pastry on top of the mixture, dampening the edges underneath and pressing down. Trim the excess, re-roll and cut out decorations. Cut two holes in the top to allow the steam to escape. Refrigerate the pie until you are ready to cook. Brush the pastry with the egg yolk and cook in the centre of a preheated oven, Gas Mark 6/200°C/400°F for about 25 minutes.
Serves 6–8

▲ *Root vegetable pie with parsnip pastry*

GREEN BEANS WITH SHIITAKE MUSHROOMS, CHILLI AND SPRING ONIONS

If garlic shoots are available, substitute them for the spring onions in this Vietnamese-style dish.

2–3 generous handfuls of lambs'
*   lettuce or 1 curly lettuce*
2 handfuls of bean sprouts
Bunch of fresh mint leaves
625–750g (1¼–1½lb) green beans
150g (5oz) spring onions
1–2 fresh red chillies
25g (1oz) butter
2 tablespoons groundnut oil
150g (5oz) shiitake mushrooms,
*   thinly sliced*
Salt

Arrange the lettuce leaves, bean sprouts and mint leaves together in a large shallow serving dish, overlapping the edge. Top and tail the beans and cut them in half if very long. Slice the spring onions across in 5mm (¼-inch) pieces. Cut the chillies in half under running water, discard the seeds and stem and then slice across very thinly. Either steam the green beans or boil them in plenty of salted water for only a few minutes until they are soft but still bright green. Unless you are ready to eat at once, run the beans under cold water and put to one side.

Just before you are ready to eat, put

the butter and oil into a wok or large frying pan over a high heat. When the butter has melted, add the sliced mushrooms and toss them for 3–4 minutes, then add the spring onions, beans and chilli. Stir for about two minutes or until the spring onions have softened but are still bright green. Sprinkle the mushroom mixture with salt, turn it out on to the dish of leaves and serve at once.
TO SERVE As a main dish, serve this with cooked potatoes or noodles tossed in a wok with butter, sesame oil, chopped garlic and fresh coriander.
Serves 6

AUBERGINE CRUMBLE

This versatile dish can also be eaten as a first course or as a side dish.

2 large aubergines
125g (4oz) strong Cheddar cheese,
*   grated finely*
50g (2oz) butter
2 tablespoons olive oil
2 teaspoons sesame oil
75g (3oz) fresh wholemeal or
*   granary breadcrumbs*
1 tablespoon chopped fresh dill
Salt and black pepper

Set the oven to preheat at Gas Mark 3/160°C/325°F. Put the aubergines under the hottest possible grill, turning them once or twice, until they are burnt and even cracked outside, and feel soft and collapsed inside. When they are cool enough to handle, slit them open and, using a metal spoon, scrape out the interior flesh into a sieve. Press out all the liquid using the back of a wooden spoon. Put the drained flesh into a food processor with 75g (3oz) of the grated cheese and all the butter.

Whizz the aubergine mixture to a purée and then, still whizzing, slowly pour in the olive and sesame oils. Season to taste and turn out the mixture into a shallow, ovenproof dish.

Mix the breadcrumbs with the remaining cheese and spread on top of the purée. Dribble a little olive oil over the top and cook on a high shelf for 30–45 minutes or until the top is browned. Before serving, scatter the chopped dill over the top.
Serves 6

BAKED FENNEL AND SHALLOTS WITH WARM SPICY DRESSING

This spicy, aromatic dish is wonderful eaten with bread and cheese for a light lunch or supper.

5 large fennel bulbs
8 shallots, peeled
1 rounded teaspoon caster sugar
1 bunch of spring onions
3 tablespoons olive oil
1 tablespoon sesame oil
2.5–5cm (1–2-inch) piece of fresh
*   root ginger, finely chopped*
2 large garlic cloves, chopped finely
2 tablespoons lemon juice
3 pinches of chilli powder
Salt and black pepper
Fresh sprigs of fennel, to garnish

Set the oven to preheat at Gas Mark 3/160°C/325°F. Cut off the base, stalks and any marked outer parts of the fennel. Quarter the four largest bulbs lengthways and arrange them in a shallow ovenproof dish. Scatter the shallots among the fennel. Season with black pepper and a little salt and sprinkle the top evenly with caster sugar. Cover the dish with foil and cook in the centre of the oven for about 1½ hours until both vegetables are soft.

Meanwhile, cut the spring onions across in 5mm (¼-inch) pieces, using the green part as well. Chop the remaining fennel very finely. When the fennel and shallots are cooked, put the

olive and sesame oils into a large, deep frying pan over a medium heat, add the ginger and garlic and stir for two minutes; then add the spring onions and stir for a further minute. Finally, add the chopped fennel and the lemon juice, stir together and remove from the heat. Season with the chilli powder and salt. Spoon the dressing over the baked fennel and garnish with sprigs of fennel to serve.
Serves 4

▶ *Green beans with shiitake mushrooms, chilli and spring onions; aubergine crumble; baked fennel and shallots with warm spicy dressing*

POTATO AND TOMATO GRATINÉE WITH ANCHOVIES AND YOGURT

This simple dish is a pleasure to make and can be made ahead of time and then kept warm in a low oven. If you are totally vegetarian, you can leave out the anchovies but add a little more salt. It is also now possible to get vegetarian Parmesan if you prefer.

750g (1½lb) potatoes, peeled
625–750g (1¼–1½lb) tomatoes
50g (2oz) can of anchovy fillets
4 large garlic cloves, sliced thinly
Caster sugar, to sprinkle
1 rounded tablespoon cornflour
2 tablespoons milk
450ml (¾ pint) Greek-style yogurt
40–50g (1½–2oz) Parmesan cheese, grated coarsely
Salt and black pepper

Steam or boil the potatoes until they are cooked but not falling apart. Drain and cool them slightly, then slice them fairly thinly across. Put the tomatoes in a bowl and cover them with boiling water. Drain the tomatoes, peel off the skins and slice them fairly thickly across. Drain the anchovies and cut them into small pieces. Set the oven to preheat at Gas Mark 4/180°C/350°F.

Generously butter a large, shallow, rectangular or round ovenproof dish. Put a layer of potato slices on the bottom of the dish, sprinkle them with some of the anchovy and garlic pieces and follow with a layer of tomato slices and a sprinkling of caster sugar. Continue alternating in this way, ending with a layer of potatoes.

Put the cornflour in a saucepan, add the milk and stir until smooth. Stir in the yogurt, then place the saucepan over the heat and bring to the boil, stirring in one direction only. Allow the mixture to bubble, still stirring, for 2–3 minutes to stabilize the yogurt so that it doesn't curdle later while in the oven. Finally, season with a little salt and plenty of black pepper and spoon the yogurt evenly all over the potato and tomato mixture in the dish.

Sprinkle the grated Parmesan cheese over the top of the dish and cook towards the top of the preheated oven for 45–60 minutes, or until the top of the gratinée is speckled brown all over. Serve immediately while still warm.
Serves 6

SWEET RED PEPPERS
STUFFED WITH MINTED AUBERGINE PURÉE

Ever since I started travelling in Turkey at the age of 18, I have loved aubergine purées of all kinds. The pale, light filling in this dish, combined with fromage frais, garlic and mint, enhances the delicate taste of the cucumber. If you want to prepare this dish for a vegan, you can replace the fromage frais with tahini, which is a smooth nutty purée of sesame seeds. This filling could also be used very successfully in a pitta bread filling or as a dip.

3 red peppers
800g (1lb 10oz) aubergines
2 tablespoons lemon juice
250g (8oz) natural fromage frais
1 garlic clove, crushed
1 teaspoon caster sugar
2–3 pinches of chilli powder
1 rounded tablespoon finely chopped fresh mint
Salt
TO GARNISH:
Small leaves of fresh mint
Chopped mint
Extra chilli powder, to sprinkle

◄ Potato and tomato gratinée with anchovies and yogurt

Cut the pepper in half lengthways and carefully remove the seeds and white pith. Put the halves into a saucepan of boiling salted water and simmer for 10 minutes. Drain and stuff each pepper half with a roughly crumpled ball of silver foil. Place a large glassful of water in a roasting pan, put the peppers in the pan and cook them in the centre of a preheated oven, Gas Mark 4/180°C/350°F, for 30–40 minutes, or until they are soft.

Meanwhile, put the aubergines under a very hot grill for about 20 minutes, turning once or twice until the skin is charred black all over. As they will be very hot, peel off the skin under cold water, put the flesh into a strainer and press the flesh down firmly with a wooden spoon to squeeze out as much liquid as possible. Put the hot flesh into a food processor, adding the lemon juice, fromage frais, garlic, caster sugar, chilli powder and a little salt. Whizz until smooth, then turn the mixture out into a bowl and leave to cool. Stir in the chopped mint.

When the peppers are cooked, take them out of the oven and leave them to cool. Remove the foil. Put the peppers

onto individual serving plates and spoon the purée into them. Sprinkle on a pinch of chilli powder and decorate with chopped and whole mint leaves.
Serves 6

▲ Sweet red peppers stuffed with minted aubergine purée

HOT CHESTNUT AND SPINACH TERRINE WITH RED CHILLI

I make this dish as a winter main course. Both chestnuts and spinach are particularly enhanced by fresh ginger, and the slivers of chilli give the terrine a lovely bite. Use the left-over egg yolks for a lovely rich sponge cake or for homemade mayonnaise.

1 large plump red chilli
675g (1½lb) spinach, trimmed
5cm (2-inch) piece of fresh root
*   ginger, chopped finely*
3–4 garlic cloves, chopped finely
Finely grated zest of 1 orange
125g (4oz) unsalted butter
Bunch of flat leaf parsley
1 large egg (size 1)
4 egg whites
375–425g (12–14oz) vacuum
*   packed or canned whole chestnuts*
Salt

Cut the chilli in half under running water and discard the seeds and stem. Cut the chilli flesh across into very thin short strips. Bring a little salted water to the boil, add the washed spinach, cover and boil the spinach until the leaves are soft. Drain the spinach well and press out as much liquid as possible with the back of a spoon. To dry the spinach thoroughly, pat the leaves between kitchen paper. Put the spinach into a food processor and add the ginger and garlic and the orange zest. Sprinkle quite generously with salt as it will be diluted by the eggs later. Add the butter and whizz until finely puréed. Leave the mixture to cool for about 10 minutes. Put a large roasting pan of hot water in the centre of the oven and heat the oven to Gas Mark 3/160°C/325°F.

Line the sides of a 1.2-litre (2-pint) tin or terrine dish with buttered baking parchment. Scatter the chilli strips over the base and also up the sides by pressing them against the buttered paper. Then press on several good sprigs of flat leaf parsley. Add the egg and egg whites to the spinach purée in the food processor and whizz thoroughly. Add extra salt to taste if needed. Leave the mixture to cool completely.

Add the chestnuts to the purée and mix in gently. Spoon the mixture carefully into the prepared tin so as not to disarrange the strips of chilli and the sprigs of parsley. Butter a large piece of foil and place it loosely on top, but pressing the edges to seal. Pierce two or three holes in the foil to allow the steam to escape. Put the tin into the water in the roasting pan and cook for 1¼-1½ hours or until a small knife inserted in the centre comes out clean. If you are eating immediately, remove it from the heat and leave for a few minutes. Then put the tin upside down against an oblong serving dish, giving it a good shake to turn the terrine out. *TO SERVE* Carefully remove the baking parchment and serve warm, accompanied by a frisée salad with added walnuts and good bread or new potatoes.
Serves 4–6

NEW POTATOES WITH GREEN LENTILS AND SPRING ONIONS

This is a nutritious dish which you can serve as a main course accompanied by green vegetables or a salad. It can be prepared quickly in advance and then it needs only a minute or two last-minute cooking in a wok. When I first made this, the countryside was full of wild garlic; the star-like white flowers thrown on to this dish looked very pretty and tasted good too. If garlic shoots are available, try substituting them for the chives.

75g (3oz) green lentils
500g (1lb) small waxy new potatoes
6–8 spring onions
Generous handful of chives
4 tablespoons extra virgin olive oil
2 tablespoons balsamic vinegar
Sea salt
Black pepper

◄ *Hot chestnut and spinach terrine with red chilli*

Bring a large saucepan of salted water to the boil. Rinse the lentils thoroughly, then cook them in the boiling water for 15–30 minutes or until tender. Drain the lentils and leave on one side. Meanwhile, either steam or boil the potatoes until they are just soft right through, then drain and cut them in half, unless they are really small. Trim the base from the spring onions. Cut the chives and spring onions across in strips of about 7.5cm (3 inches), using as much of the green part of the spring onion as possible.

Just before serving, put the olive oil in a wok over a high heat, then add the lentils, potatoes, spring onions and chives. Toss the mixture over the high heat for a few minutes or until the spring onions and chives are bright green and just softened. Season the mixture well with sea salt and plenty of black pepper. Toss the vegetables once more and turn them out into a heated serving dish. Sprinkle the balsamic vinegar over the top.
Serves 3–4

▲ *New potatoes with green lentils and spring onions*

SPINACH, PARSLEY AND SORREL PURÉE WITH BALSAMIC BRAISED LEEKS

Serve this either as one of several vegetarian dishes for a main course; or make it into a main dish itself by adding thin slivers of skinless chicken breast to the braised leeks when they are cooked. Simply stir the chicken around with the leeks for a few minutes until all the liquid has evaporated.

500g–750g (1–1½lb) small thin
leeks, trimmed
3 tablespoons olive oil
5–6 tablespoons balsamic vinegar
500g (1lb) spinach
Large bunch of parsley
Generous handful of sorrel leaves
50g (2oz) butter
Finely grated zest of ½ orange
Salt and black pepper

Cut the leeks across into 5cm (2-inch) pieces, then wash and drain. Put the olive oil into a wide, heavy saucepan or a deep sauté pan over a low heat. Add the leeks, cover the pan and cook very gently until they begin to soften. Then remove the lid, add three tablespoons of the balsamic vinegar and continue cooking the leeks gently in the open pan, stirring now and then, for 20–30 minutes. Add the remaining vinegar at separate intervals until the leeks are very soft and browned, and the balsamic juices have almost evaporated. Season the mixture to taste with salt and plenty of freshly ground black pepper.

While the leeks are cooking, prepare the spinach purée. Either steam or boil the spinach in a little water for a few minutes until just soft, then add the parsley and cook for another minute. Finally add the sorrel leaves and stir until the leaves go limp and lose their bright green colour. Drain the leaves very well, pressing out any excess liquid with the back of a spoon. Put the mixture into a food processor with the butter and grated orange zest. Whizz until smoothly puréed. Season the purée to taste with salt and black pepper and spoon it out into a wide gratinée or serving dish. Cover loosely with foil and keep the dish warm in a very low oven until the leeks are ready. Arrange the leeks on top of the spinach and serve immediately.
Serves 6

ROOT VEGETABLE MOUSSE WITH HONEYED TOP

The combination of creamy sweet carrots, parsnips and a hint of peppery turnip in this chilled mousse is an unexpected pleasure. Cold mousses are always popular for buffets.

FOR THE MOUSSE:
250g (8oz) carrots, chopped roughly
250g (8oz) parsnips, chopped
roughly
300ml (½ pint) double cream
2 eggs
¼ whole nutmeg, grated
Salt
Chilli powder
FOR THE TOPPING:
3 tablespoons sherry vinegar
2 rounded tablespoons honey
5 tablespoons extra virgin olive oil
1 large garlic clove, sliced finely
1 large carrot, cut into thin strips
1 turnip, cut into thin strips
2–3 sprigs of flat leaf parsley, to
garnish
Salt
Black pepper

◀ *Spinach, parsley and sorrel purée with balsamic braised leeks*

Smear a deep 15cm (6-inch) diameter cake tin with olive oil and put a piece of oiled baking parchment in the bottom. Set the oven to preheat at Gas Mark 2/150°C/300°F.

To make the mousse, boil both the carrots and parsnips in salted water until soft. Drain the vegetables and put them into a food processor. Add the cream and eggs and whizz until very smooth. Whizz in the nutmeg with a little salt and chilli powder to taste. Spoon the mixture into the prepared cake tin. Cook the mousse just below the centre of the preheated oven for 50–60 minutes, or until the mousse is just firm to a light touch in the centre. Then remove the mousse from the oven and leave it until cold. Meanwhile, make the honey and vegetable topping.

Put the sherry vinegar, honey and olive oil in a saucepan over a medium heat, stirring to dissolve the honey. When the honey has melted, add the sliced garlic, carrots and turnips and stir over the heat for 4–5 minutes. Season the vegetable mixture to taste with salt and black pepper and leave it until cold. When the mousse is cold, carefully loosen the sides with a knife. Turn the mousse out on to a serving plate. Remove the disc of baking parchment and refrigerate the mousse until you are ready to eat.
TO SERVE Spoon the topping on to the mousse and garnish with parsley.
Serves 4

▲ *Root vegetable mousse with honeyed top*

TUE'S MOTHER'S VEGETABLE DISH

Tue was my guide on a recent visit to Hue in Vietnam. This dish, based on one made by his mother, can be adapted by adding slivers of chicken or fish.

2 fresh red chillies
1 bunch of spring onions
75g (3oz) coconut milk powder or
*   175g (6oz) creamed coconut*
1 rounded teaspoon salt
600ml (1 pint) very hot water
1 Cos lettuce
1cm (½-inch) piece of root ginger
3 large garlic cloves
300g (10oz) cherry tomatoes
175g (6oz) shiitake mushrooms
125g (4oz) fresh baby corn
250g (8oz) canned water chestnuts
Handful of fresh mint leaves
Handful of fresh coriander leaves
4–5 Thai lime leaves (optional)
2 handfuls of small spinach leaves
250g (8oz) bean sprouts
8 tablespoons lemon juice
2 tablespoons groundnut oil

Prepare all the ingredients before you start to cook. Cut the chillies open lengthways under running water, discard the seeds and stem and then slice the flesh across as thinly as possible. Prepare the spring onions by trimming the tops and bottoms, and cut them across in 5mm (¼-inch) pieces, using as much of the green part as possible. Put the coconut milk powder or creamed coconut and the salt into a measuring jug, add the very hot water and stir until the coconut has dissolved completely. Slice the Cos lettuce across in 2.5cm (1-inch) strips. Finely chop the fresh root ginger and the garlic. Halve the cherry tomatoes. Slice the shiitake mushrooms across thinly. Slice the baby corn in half lengthways. Drain the canned water chestnuts and cut into slices about the thickness of a pound coin. Roughly chop the fresh mint and coriander leaves. Finely chop the Thai lime leaves, if you are using them. Have ready the spinach leaves,

the bean sprouts and the lemon juice.

To cook, heat the groundnut oil in a wok or a large heavy casserole dish over a high heat. Add the shiitake mushrooms and stir for 1–2 minutes until they begin to soften. Then stir in the chopped ginger and garlic and the Thai lime leaves (if using), followed by the chopped chillies. Immediately add the halved cherry tomatoes, the baby corn and the water chestnuts and then pour in the coconut milk.

Bring the mixture to the boil, bubble in the open pan for no more than two minutes, then add the sliced spring onions and bean sprouts. Next add the sliced lettuce and spinach leaves and stir in until they are just wilted. Finally, stir in the lemon juice followed by the chopped mint and coriander leaves, and then serve immediately.
TO SERVE Serve this dish with an accompaniment of Chinese noodles or rice to mop up the milky juices.
Serves 4

HOT STUFFED AVOCADOS WITH MOZZARELLA CHEESE

This light meal of avocados, filled with a mixture of sweet pepper purée and tomatoes, and topped with melted cheese is extremely good. Use really large avocados, and plum tomatoes if they are available, as their flavour is so much better for cooking. This dish will serve eight people for a first course. If you want a special treat, get the authentic Italian *mozzarella di bufala*, made with buffalo milk.

1 red pepper, chopped roughly
3 large unpeeled garlic cloves
1 tablespoon lemon juice
2 teaspoons caster sugar
2 tomatoes
10–12 fresh basil or mint leaves,
*   sliced thinly*
4 large ripe avocados
1 mozzarella cheese, sliced thinly
Salt
Black pepper

Set the oven to preheat at Gas Mark 5/190°C/375°F. Put the chopped red pepper into a saucepan of boiling water with the unpeeled garlic and simmer for about 10 minutes. Drain and put the pepper and garlic into a processor, discarding the garlic skins which should have popped off during boiling. Add most of the lemon juice, reserving just a little. Season with salt, black pepper and sugar. Whizz until smooth and turn the mixture into a bowl.

Put the tomatoes into a bowl and cover them with boiling water. Leave them for one minute, then peel and chop the flesh into small pieces. Stir the chopped tomatoes and basil or mint into the red purée. Halve and stone the avocados and smear the flesh with the reserved lemon juice to prevent discoloration.

Put the avocado halves in a shallow ovenproof dish and fill the hollow with the pepper and tomato mixture.

Arrange the slices of mozzarella on

to the pepper stuffing and around the edges of the avocados. Cook the avocados in the centre of the oven for 10–15 minutes. Serve immediately.
Serves 4

▲ *Hot stuffed avocados with mozzarella cheese*

◀ *Tue's mother's vegetable dish*

Leek and red onion cobbler with potato and cheese pastry

Everyone loves this combination of tastes. Leeks are one of my favourite vegetables, especially when covered in this light, potato pastry. As an alternative to leeks, you can use bulb fennel.

For the filling:
   1kg (2lb) leeks
   2 large red onions
   25g (1oz) butter
   4 tablespoons extra virgin olive oil
   2 teaspoons caraway seeds
   4–5 pinches of chilli powder
   Sea salt

For the pastry top:
   375g (12oz) potatoes
   175g (6oz) self-raising flour
   1 rounded teaspoon salt
   75g (3oz) strong flavoured grated cheese
   150g (5oz) butter
   1 egg yolk
   1 tablespoon grated Parmesan

To make the filling, trim the leeks and cut into 2.5cm (1-inch) pieces, using as much of the green part as possible. Peel the onions and chop into roughly 2.5cm (1-inch) pieces. Melt the butter with the olive oil in a large, deep frying pan. Add the leeks and onions and caraway seeds. Cook over a medium heat, stirring fairly often, until the leeks and onions have softened. Season to taste with the chilli powder and salt. Turn the filling into a large, shallow, ovenproof dish. Leave to cool while you make the pastry.

For the pastry, peel the potatoes. Steam or boil them until they are soft. Mash them in a bowl until they are as smooth as possible. Leave the mashed potatoes until cold. Sift together the flour and salt into another bowl. Stir in the grated cheese. Then add the butter, cut into small pieces, and rub with your finger tips until the mixture resembles rough breadcrumbs. Work in the cold mashed potato with your hands and knead the mixture to make a smooth dough. If you are not using the dough immediately, form it into a ball, wrap it in clingfilm and refrigerate.

When the leek mixture is cold, roll the pastry out to about 5mm (¼-inch) thick on a floured board. Using a 6cm (2½-inch) biscuit cutter, cut the pastry into circles, re-rolling the scraps. Arrange the circles overlapping on top of the leek mixture. The dish can be refrigerated at this point until you are ready to cook.

To cook, preheat the oven to Gas Mark 6/200°C/400°F. Brush the pastry circles with egg yolk and then sprinkle with the grated Parmesan cheese. Cook the cobbler in the centre of the oven for 25–30 minutes until the pastry has turned a rich golden brown.
Serves 6

Garden Pie

One of the difficulties of making good vegetarian main dishes is how to make them substantial enough without them being rather stodgy. Pies are often a satisfactory solution. This is a lovely fresh-tasting pie which you can decorate to look pretty and inviting. Try and use plum tomatoes if they are available, as their flavour is much better. Serve this dish with new potatoes and a salad.

   375g (12oz) tomatoes
   250g (8oz) small courgettes
   125g (4oz) baby corn
   125g (4oz) frozen petits pois
   125g (4oz) bean sprouts
   1 large garlic clove, chopped finely
   1 sprig of fresh tarragon, chopped roughly
   2 egg yolks
   300ml (½ pint) double cream
   400g (13oz) frozen puff pastry
   Salt
   Black pepper

◄ *Leek and red onion cobbler with potato and cheese pastry*

Put the tomatoes into a bowl, cover with boiling water and leave for one minute. Skin and cut them into small pieces. Slice the courgettes across very finely. Slice the baby corn thinly lengthways. Put the petits pois into a strainer and pour water over them just to thaw them. Put the prepared vegetables, bean sprouts, garlic and tarragon into a buttered, fairly shallow ovenproof dish, Put the egg yolks into a bowl and whisk in the cream. Season the cream well and pour it over the vegetables.

Roll out the pastry into a piece big enough to fit the top of the dish. Moisten the edges of the dish, lay the pastry on top and press gently around the edge to seal. Cut the pastry edges off neatly. Re-roll the scraps of pastry and cut out shapes for decoration. Moisten the underside of the shapes and arrange them on the pie. Cut two small holes in the centre of the pie to allow the steam to escape. If there is time, chill the pie in the refrigerator for at least 30 minutes before baking. Set the oven to preheat at Gas Mark 6/200°C/400°F. Brush the pie lightly with a little milk and cook it just above the centre of the oven for about 30 minutes or until the pastry is puffed and a rich brown.
Serves 4

▲ *Garden pie*

BLANQUETTE OF CHICORY, TURNIPS AND SHALLOTS WITH HONEY AND MUSTARD

This lovely creamy casserole has a tantalizing fusion of flavours; sweet, peppery and slightly bitter all at once.

6 large chicory
25g (1oz) butter
3 tablespoons olive oil
500g (1lb) baby turnips, trimmed
375g (12oz) shallots, peeled
8 juniper berries, crushed roughly
2 rounded tablespoons plain flour
450ml (¾ pint) milk
300ml (½ pint) double cream
1 tablespoon honey
5 teaspoons coarse grain mustard
2 tablespoons lemon juice
2 egg yolks
Generous handful of fresh dill,
*   chopped roughly*
Salt and black pepper

Set the oven to preheat at Gas Mark 3/160°C/325°F. Cut just the very bottom off the whole chicory. Gently melt the butter with the olive oil in a large casserole on top of the stove. Remove the casserole from the heat and add the turnips, shallots and chicory. Stir with a wooden spoon to coat the vegetables with the butter and oil. Add the crushed juniper berries. Then stir in the flour thoroughly.

Put the milk and 150ml (¼ pint) of the cream into a saucepan with the honey and mustard. Season with salt and black pepper. Place the pan over a medium heat, stirring until the honey has dissolved. Pour the heated milk and cream into the casserole and stir. Put the casserole back over a fairly high heat and bring the mixture to the boil, stirring gently all the time until the liquid thickens. Then cover the casserole and cook in the centre of the oven for one hour, or until the vegetables are really soft.

Remove the casserole from the oven and stir in the lemon juice. Put the remaining cream into a bowl with the egg yolks and whisk lightly together with a fork. Then stir the cream into the casserole. Taste the mixture and add more seasoning or mustard if you like. Before serving, put the casserole back over a medium heat on top of the stove to reheat, without boiling. Lastly, stir the chopped dill into the casserole.
TO SERVE Serve with new potatoes and a green vegetable, such as spring greens or cabbage.
Serves 6

BEETROOT TART WITH CREAM CHEESE AND CARAWAY PASTRY

For a light lunch or supper, this scarlet upside-down beetroot tart looks beautiful when it is accompanied by a green mixed leaf salad. The crumbly, crusty cream cheese pastry is extremely easy and takes only a few minutes to make, and its flavour and texture contrast well with the smooth slices of cooked beetroot. You can make the tart in advance and reheat it, still in its dish, or, if you prefer, you can cook the tart and keep it warm in a very low oven until you are ready to serve.

75g (3oz) full-fat soft cheese
125g (4oz) unsalted butter
2 teaspoons caraway seeds
175g (6oz) plain flour
2 teaspoons baking powder
3 generous pinches of chilli powder
625g (1¼lb) cooked and skinned
*   small fresh beetroot, sliced thinly*
*   (approximately)*
Salt
Black pepper
Sprigs of flat-leafed parsley, to
*   garnish*

◀ *Blanquette of chicory, turnips and shallots with honey and mustard*

Put the cream cheese and 75g (3oz) of the butter into a food processor and whizz briefly to mix together. Then add the caraway seeds, flour, baking powder, chilli powder and a good sprinkling of salt. Whizz once again to form a dough. Pat the dough into a ball, wrap it in clingfilm and refrigerate the dough for about 20 minutes.

Set the oven to preheat at Gas Mark 6/200°C/400°F. Smear the bottom of a 23cm (9-inch) earthenware flan dish with the remaining butter and sprinkle it evenly with salt and a little black pepper. Lay the beetroot slices in a neatly overlapping layer on the bottom of the flan dish. Continue layering with the remaining beetroot. Roll out the cold dough on a lightly floured surface into a circle very slightly bigger than the flan dish. Lay the pastry on top of the beetroot and press the edges down the inner sides of the flan dish, making a thick rim. Pierce two small holes in the pastry with a skewer to allow the steam to escape. Cook the tart on the centre shelf of the oven for about 30 minutes or until the pastry is browned.

Remove the tart from the oven and leave it to cool for 8–10 minutes. Then turn it out on a flat serving plate by giving the flan dish a shake against the plate before carefully lifting it off the tart.
TO SERVE Garnish the top of the tart with a few perfect sprigs of flat-leafed parsley and serve the tart warm. If you like, you can serve a bowl of natural yogurt, seasoned with salt and coarsely ground black pepper, as a sauce.
Serves 4

▲ *Beetroot tart with cream cheese and caraway pastry*

PUDDINGS & CAKES

There is no doubt that eating large quantities of puddings and cakes does neither your figure or your teeth much good, but there is also no doubt that making and eating them is a therapeutic activity and can make you feel happier. To me, Sunday lunch without a pudding seems not to be the real thing at all and a sweet surprise at the end of a dinner party certainly makes the most appreciated finale. However, though there is so much scope in this area of cooking, it seems to leave many people at a loss. You do have to balance puddings well with the rest of the meal; a rich and substantial pudding after a heavy main course is clearly a mistake. But a sharp sorbet might be just the thing. Equally after a delicate fish dish, a buttery crusted tart or something chocolaty can be perfect. A cosy tea with a good cake is to me even more of an indulgence, and a real treat. The ingredients for cake-making are a great pleasure to work with and what happens to cakes once put in the oven always seems a miracle. And as for the eating; well, I can't remember ever being able to restrict myself to eating only one slice of a freshly made cake.

FROMAGE FRAIS AND DARK CHOCOLATE ICE CREAM CAKE

The chocolate layers of this dramatic and delectable party piece are a cooked flourless cake. The fromage frais ice cream is like a very light cheesecake. Although I make this with marmalade, apricot jam is an excellent alternative.

FOR THE CHOCOLATE LAYERS:
  3 tablespoons water
  150g (5oz) darkest bitter chocolate, broken into pieces
  4 large eggs (size 1)
  150g (5oz) caster sugar
  ½ teaspoon salt
  2 tablespoons thin-shred marmalade or apricot jam
FOR THE ICE CREAM:
  2 egg whites
  1 teaspoon salt
  175ml (6 fl oz) water
  175g (6oz) caster sugar
  200g (7oz) virtually fat-free fromage frais
  25g (1oz) chocolate, grated

◄ *Fromage frais and dark chocolate ice cream cake*

Make the chocolate layers in advance. Line two 22–23cm (8½–9-inch) sandwich tins with a piece of baking parchment and preheat the oven to Gas Mark 4/180°C/350°F. Put the water into a double boiler or a bowl set over a pan of very hot but not boiling water. Add the chocolate. Occasionally stir until the chocolate has melted. Remove the pan from the heat. Now separate the eggs into two large bowls. Add the sugar to the egg yolks and whisk them until pale. Then add the melted chocolate and whisk again until smooth. Add the salt to the egg whites and whisk until they hold soft peaks. Fold the egg whites into the chocolate mixture with a metal spoon and spread the mixture evenly in the sandwich tins. Cook in the centre of the oven for about 20 minutes, or until the cakes are firm to touch. Leave to cool in the tins.

When the cakes are cold, loosen the edges of one cake with a knife. Turn it out on to a wide serving plate and remove the paper. Spread the cake thinly with one tablespoon of the marmalade. To make the ice cream, put the egg whites into a bowl with the salt and whisk until they hold soft peaks. Put the water and caster sugar into a saucepan. Stir over a low heat to dissolve the sugar, then bring the mixture to the boil and boil fiercely, without stirring, for three minutes. Then pour the syrup on to the whisked egg whites in a thin stream, whisking all the time. Continue whisking until the mixture is cold and stiff. Gently fold in the fromage frais. Spread half the mixture in a thick layer on top of the marmalade-coated chocolate layer.

Loosen the edges of the second cake, turn it out on to a flat surface, then spread it with the remaining marmalade. Place the cake on top of the layer of ice cream. Spread the remaining ice cream evenly over the top. Finally, sprinkle the grated chocolate on top. Freeze the cake for several hours. An hour before eating, take the cake out of the freezer and put it into the main part of the refrigerator to soften slightly.

UPSIDE-DOWN APPLE TART
WITH ORANGE AND OATMEAL PASTRY

This upside-down tart combines sliced apples with the wonderfully compatible flavours of cardamom, honey and orange, and the fine oatmeal gives the pastry a delicious nutty crunch. The tart can be made in advance, kept in the baking tin and reheated. I occasionally use a shallow heart-shaped tin which looks especially pretty for a party. If you can find them, quinces make a particularly good substitute for the apples but they will need to be cooked for a little while longer.

125g (4oz) plain flour
50g (2oz) fine oatmeal
75g (3oz) caster sugar
¼ teaspoon salt
125g (4oz) butter
Finely grated zest of 1 orange
1–2 tablespoons freshly squeezed
  orange juice
750g (1½lb) dessert apples
4 tablespoons lemon juice
2 tablespoons fine-cut orange
  marmalade
2 tablespoons clear honey
Seeds of 4–5 cardamom pods,
  ground finely

To make the pastry, put the flour, oatmeal, caster sugar and salt into a food processor and whizz just once to mix. Cut the butter into small pieces, add to the flour mixture in the food processor and whizz again only briefly, just until the mixture resembles rough breadcrumbs. Add the finely grated orange zest and, with the motor running, pour in enough orange juice, whizzing very briefly, for the dough to begin to stick together. Pat the pastry into a ball, cover it with clingfilm and leave it in the refrigerator to chill while you prepare the apples.

Smear the base and sides of a 19–20cm (7½–8-inch) sandwich tin with a little butter (don't use a tin with a loose base) and preheat the oven to Gas Mark 6/200°C/400°F. Peel the apples, and, using a very sharp knife, cut each apple in half and cut out the cores. Slice the apples thinly in half moon slices, putting the slices into a bowl and sprinkling them immediately with lemon juice as you cut them to prevent them discolouring. Put the marmalade and honey into a bowl with the ground cardamom seeds, stir

together, and spread the mixture over the bottom of the buttered sandwich tin. Next, arrange the apple slices neatly overlapping in the tin.

Take the pastry from the refrigerator and, using a well floured rolling pin, roll it out very lightly on a floured board to the size of the cake tin. Carefully roll back the pastry over the rolling pin and place it on top of the apples in the tin. If the pastry should break at all, don't worry, simply press it together again. Press the overlapping pastry edge down into the sides of the tin and pierce two holes in the top to allow the steam to escape.

Cook the tart in the centre of the preheated oven for 25 minutes, then turn down to Gas Mark 3/160°C/325°F for 30 minutes. Finally, turn off the oven, open the door slightly and leave the tart in the oven for a further 10–15 minutes.

TO SERVE Slide a knife around the edges of the tin and carefully turn the tart out on to a flat serving plate. Serve the tart warm with crème fraîche, cream or natural yogurt.
Serves 8

APRICOT, ROSEMARY AND HONEY SOUFFLÉ

Some puddings are truly divine, and this is one of them. It is a light, chilled soufflé with the wonderful intense flavour of apricots, excitingly enhanced with fresh rosemary. It is marvellously refreshing after a rich meal. You can make it in one large soufflé dish or in six individual ramekin dishes.

375g (12oz) fresh apricots, chopped
  finely
3 tablespoons clear honey
8 tablespoons lemon juice
2 rounded teaspoons finely chopped
  fresh rosemary
3 teaspoons gelatine or
  3 tablespoons agar-agar flakes
4 large eggs (size 1), separated
Pinch of salt
Sprigs of rosemary, to garnish

Put the chopped apricots into a saucepan with the honey, lemon juice and chopped rosemary. Bring the mixture to the boil, stirring as the honey melts, then simmer gently, stirring now and then, for 15–20 minutes or until the apricots are completely soft. Remove the pan from the heat and add the gelatine powder or agar-agar flakes to the mixture. Refer to the instructions on the packet to ensure that the gelatine powder or agar-agar flakes dissolve thoroughly before continuing.

Place the egg yolks in a pudding basin set over a pan of barely simmering water. Using a wooden spoon, stir the apricot mixture briskly into the egg yolks. Continue stirring for about five minutes or until the mixture

thickens slightly. Then remove the bowl from the heat and leave the mixture to one side until it has cooled.

When the mixture is cool, place the egg whites into a large bowl, add the salt and whisk until the egg whites hold soft peaks. Using a large metal spoon, fold them gently but thoroughly into the apricot and egg yolk mixture. Pour the mixture into individual dishes or a single serving bowl.

Put a small sprig of rosemary in the centre of each individual dish and chill in the refrigerator for at least two hours before serving.
Serves 6

▶ *Upside-down apple tart with orange and oatmeal pastry; apricot, rosemary and honey soufflé*

RASPBERRY AND ORANGE PARFAIT IN A CHOCOLATE CASE

Years ago, I invented a chocolate case like this for a lemon soufflé. It was such a success that I have done it many times, using different shapes and fillings. This is one of the best. The case is filled with an especially light ice cream. When you can't get raspberries, you can use strawberries instead, and for the best results, use blood orange juice if it's available. Although this recipe uses white chocolate you can also use dark chocolate. In either case, use the chocolate with the highest cocoa solid content you can find, and no lower than 50%.

FOR THE CHOCOLATE CASE:
  175g (6oz) white chocolate
  1 tablespoon water
  15g (½oz) unsalted butter
FOR THE PARFAIT:
  500g (1lb) fresh raspberries
  2 tablespoons clear honey
  150ml (¼ pint) freshly squeezed
    orange juice
  175g (6oz) caster sugar
  2 large egg whites
  ¼ teaspoon salt
  300ml (½ pint) whipping cream
  Mint leaves, to garnish

To make the chocolate case, oil a 20cm (8-inch) deep loose-bottomed cake tin. Break up the chocolate and put it with the water into a double saucepan or a bowl set over a pan of hot, but not boiling, water. Stir until the chocolate has melted. Stir in the butter. Spoon the chocolate into the base of the tin and spread it evenly up the sides of the tin, but leaving a very uneven jagged edge. Chill the chocolate case in the refrigerator while you make the parfait.

For the parfait, remove three or four of the best raspberries for the garnish, and keep them in the refrigerator. Press the remaining raspberries through a sieve into a bowl. Stir in the clear honey and leave the purée on one side. Strain the orange juice through a strainer into a saucepan and add the sugar. Put the pan over a low heat and stir until the sugar has dissolved; then increase the heat and boil fiercely, without stirring, for three minutes exactly. Meanwhile, put the egg whites into a large bowl with the salt and, using an electric mixer, whisk until they stand in soft peaks. Immediately pour the hot orange syrup on to the whisked

egg whites, whisking all the time. Continue whisking until the mixture is as thick as an uncooked meringue. Lightly stir in the raspberry purée. Whisk the cream until it holds soft peaks, but is not stiff, and fold it into the mixture with a large metal spoon.

Pour the raspberry cream into the chilled chocolate case, piling the mixture up slightly in the centre. Freeze the parfait for at least five hours or preferably overnight.

To unmould, rub the sides of the frozen tin with a very hot cloth. Then pass a small spatula down the side of the chocolate and the tin until it has loosened all round. Put the cake tin on a jam jar and carefully push the sides of the tin down. Separate the chocolate case from the base of the tin with a spatula and carefully move it on to a serving plate. If you are not serving the dessert immediately, re-freeze it until it is needed, although you can keep it in the main part of the refrigerator for about 30 minutes. Just before serving, garnish the parfait with the reserved raspberries and the mint leaves.
Serves 6–8

BANANA, LEMON AND CARDAMOM ICE CREAM

Ever since I first went to India in 1977, I have been using cardamom for both puddings and ice creams as well as in spiced savoury dishes. It is truly a wonder spice with amazing versatility, and in puddings it can create a particularly ethereal effect.

  5 cardamom pods
  3 large eggs
  ½ teaspoon salt
  175g (6oz) demerara sugar
  6 tablespoons water
  4 large ripe bananas, chopped
    roughly
  Finely grated zest and juice of
    2 lemons
  300ml (½ pint) whipping cream

◄ *Raspberry and orange parfait in a chocolate case*

Remove the seeds from the cardamom pods and grind them finely. Put the eggs, salt and cardamom into the bowl and, using an electric mixer, whisk until frothy. Stir the sugar and water in a saucepan over a low heat until the sugar has dissolved. Then boil fiercely without stirring for three minutes. Pour this bubbling syrup in a thin stream on to the whisked eggs, whisking all the time at high speed. Continue whisking until the mixture thickens. Leave on one side to cool.

Put the bananas into a bowl or food processor with the lemon juice and grated lemon zest and mash to a purée. Stir in the cooled egg mixture. Finally, whisk the cream until it is thick but not stiff and fold it into the mixture. Pour the ice cream into a bowl and put it in the freezer for a minimum of three

hours. Move to the refrigerator to soften for half an hour before serving.
Serves 8

▲ *Banana, lemon and cardamom ice cream*

SOFT BERRY FRUITS
IN PASSION FRUIT FROMAGE FRAIS

This is a lovely creamy mixture using a selection of seasonal small berry fruits with contrasting textures and tastes, enveloped in sweetened fromage frais and enhanced by the magical scented flavour of passion fruit.

500g (1lb) 8% fat fromage frais
3 tablespoons natural Greek-style
    yogurt
40g (1½oz) icing sugar
5–6 passion fruit
4 small bananas (optional)
450g (15oz) selection seasonal
    small berry fruits
2 teaspoons clear honey

Put the fromage frais and Greek-style yogurt into a mixing bowl. Sift in the icing sugar and mix them all together thoroughly. Halve the passion fruit and scoop out the insides on to the sweetened fromage frais and yogurt mixture. Stir thoroughly to mix the passion fruit into the fromage frais. Peel the bananas, if you are using them, and cut them into small cubes. Immediately stir the banana cubes into the fromage frais mixture in the bowl.

Prepare the soft berry fruit as necessary: choose from physalis fruit, raspberries, small strawberries, blueberries, kiwifruit, even black or

white grapes; *fraises des bois* are a really special treat if you can get them. It is good to use some berry fruits with a mildly acidic taste, particularly if you are using banana; they provide a clean, sharp contrast to the luscious sweetness of the banana.

Reserve some of the prettiest fruit for decoration and mix the rest thoroughly into the passion fruit and fromage frais mixture.
TO SERVE Spoon the mixture into a pretty glass serving bowl and decorate with the reserved fruit. Drizzle the honey over the top.
Serves 6

CREAMY MARBLED BLACKBERRY
AND YOGURT MOUSSE

This jellied mousse is a delicious combination of puréed and whole fresh blackberries, mingling with a luscious mixture of natural yogurt and whipped double cream. The marbled appearance and the dark, glossy top always impresses people. If you like, the mousse can be served with pouring cream. This mousse can be made with agar-agar flakes, but the jellied top may not separate in the same way.

750g (1½lb) blackberries
8 tablespoons lemon juice
75g (3oz) caster sugar
2 tablespoons water
1 tablespoon powdered gelatine or
    agar-agar flakes
2 large egg whites (size 1)
½ teaspoon salt
300ml (½ pint) double cream
150ml (¼ pint) natural yogurt
1 tablespoon icing sugar, sifted

Pick out 250g (8oz) of the best blackberries and put on one side. Place the remainder in a pan. Add the lemon juice and caster sugar, and stir over a gentle heat until the blackberry juices

start to run. Then continue to cook them gently for a few minutes until the blackberries are quite soft. Strain the blackberries into a mixing bowl, pressing the flesh through the strainer with the back of a spoon.

Sprinkle the gelatine or agar-agar into the water over a low heat, and add the mixture to the hot fruit purée, following the packet instructions to ensure that the gelatine or agar-agar dissolves thoroughly. Leave the jelly for a while until it is cold, but is only just beginning to set.

Stir the reserved uncooked blackberries into the cold purée. In a separate, clean bowl, whisk the egg whites and salt together until they form soft peaks. Then, using a metal spoon, fold the beaten egg whites gently into the blackberry purée.

In another bowl, whisk the double cream until it is thick but has still retained its pouring consistency. Fold the yogurt and icing sugar into the whisked cream. Stir this cream only very roughly into the fruit mixture, leaving large streaks of white. Oil a 1.2-litre (2-pint) mould and pour in the unmixed purée and cream into it. Chill the mousse in the refrigerator for at least one hour or until set.

TO SERVE Before serving, turn the mousse out on to a serving plate, giving it a good shake to unmould. If necessary, dip the jelly mould briefly in a sink of hot water to loosen it. Place the mousse back in the refrigerator until you are ready to eat.
Serves 6–8

▲ *Creamy marbled blackberry and yogurt mousse*

◄ *Soft berry fruits in passion fruit fromage frais*

FROTHY PLUM AND ORANGE CARDAMOM MOUSSE

This mousse makes an interesting change from fruit fool, and it is prettier too. The mixture separates into a honeycomb mousse with a jellied top. It is best served with cream or Greek-style natural yogurt.

750g (1½lb) red plums, halved and stoned
125g (4oz) caster sugar
1 teaspoon ground cardamom
175ml (6 fl oz) fresh orange juice
4½ teaspoons gelatine or
    4 tablespoons agar-agar flakes
3 egg whites
½ teaspoon salt
Small fresh mint leaves, to garnish

Place the halved plums into a saucepan with the sugar, cardamom and two tablespoons of the orange juice. Put the pan over a fairly low heat and stir until the sugar dissolves and the plum juices begin to run. Then allow the mixture to bubble gently until the plums are really soft. Remove the pan from the heat.

In a separate pan, bring the remaining orange juice to the boil, then remove the pan from the heat, and sprinkle in the gelatine or agar-agar flakes, following the packet instructions to ensure that it dissolves thoroughly. Add the mixture to the plums. Pour the plum mixture into a processor and whizz to a fine purée.

Turn the mixture into a bowl and leave to cool.

In a clean bowl, whisk the egg whites with the salt until they hold soft peaks. Fold them gently but thoroughly into the cooled plum mixture.

Spoon the mixture into a 1.2-litre (2-pint) mould. Chill the mousse in the refrigerator for several hours until it is set. Before serving, dip the mould briefly in hot water to loosen it and turn out the mousse upside-down on to a pretty serving plate.
TO SERVE Decorate the mousse with small mint leaves, or add a small leaf to each individual serving if you prefer.
Serves 8

CHOCOLATE INSPIRATION

I have a real passion for chocolate. In my experience everyone seems to like chocolate puddings so I am always trying to think up new ones. It's important for this one that the chocolate should be as dark and bitter as possible.

175g (6oz) darkest plain chocolate
6 tablespoons water
250g (8oz) slightly stale white bread
Juice of 5 lemons
150g (5oz) demerara sugar
1 rounded tablespoon honey
3 tablespoons brandy

Line a 20cm (8-inch) sandwich tin with non-stick baking parchment, generously overlapping the edge. Break up half the chocolate into the top of a double boiler or a bowl set over a pan of hot but not boiling water — the bowl should not touch the water. Add three tablespoons of the water and stir occasionally until the chocolate is melted and smooth. Allow it to cool slightly, then pour into the parchment-lined tin. Using a spatula, spread the chocolate evenly, being sure not to leave any gaps, up the sides to the edge of the tin and over the bottom.

◀ *Frothy plum and orange cardamom mousse*

Refrigerate the tin for 30 minutes.

Meanwhile, slice the bread into thick slices and cut off the crusts. Lay the bread slices, touching each other closely, in one layer in a shallow dish. Put the lemon juice into a measuring jug and, if necessary, bring up the quantity of liquid to 450ml (¾ pint) with water. Pour the liquid into a saucepan and add the demerara sugar and the honey. Put the saucepan over a medium heat and stir until the sugar and honey have dissolved, then boil the liquid fiercely, without stirring, for two minutes. Remove the pan from the heat and stir in the brandy to taste.

Gradually spoon half the syrup evenly over the slices of bread, allowing it to absorb thoroughly. Turn the soaked slices of bread over and spoon on the remaining syrup. Leave the soaked bread on one side until it has cooled completely and absorbed all the syrup.

When the chocolate has been in the refrigerator for at least 30 minutes and the bread has absorbed the syrup, lay the bread in the chocolate case. Then break up the remaining half of the chocolate and put it into the bowl previously used with the remaining water. Set the bowl over a pan of hot water. Stir the chocolate until it is

melted and smooth; then spoon the chocolate on top of the soaked bread and spread it all over evenly and up the sides of the chocolate case to enclose the bread.

Put the tin in the freezer for about one hour; then turn the cake upside down on to a serving plate and peel off the parchment. Leave the cake at room temperature for at least one hour before serving.
Serves 6

▲ *Chocolate inspiration*

HONEY-GLAZED FRESH APRICOT TART

Fresh apricots bought in the shops have often been picked before they are ripe, and their flavour is nearly always improved by cooking. This honeyed upside-down cake (which I also make with apples) is particularly successful. The pastry is easy and does not even need rolling, as you lay thin pieces over the fruit like a patchwork and it cooks into the most delicious, buttery pastry base when the tart is turned out.

1.1kg (2½lb) fresh firm apricots
75g (3oz) fine demerara sugar
175g (6oz) plain flour
75g (3oz) icing sugar
½ teaspoon salt
125g (4oz) butter
Finely grated zest and juice of
*   1 lemon*
1 tablespoon clear honey, warmed
*   (approximately)*

Cut the apricots in half and remove the stones. Spoon the demerara sugar into a well-buttered 20cm (8-inch) earthenware flan dish and shake to an even layer on the base. Arrange a layer of apricots neatly in circles, skin side down, over the sugar in the dish. Cut any remaining apricots into smaller pieces and arrange them on top of the first layer, filling in any holes with the smallest pieces. Sift the flour, icing sugar and salt into a bowl. Melt the butter in a saucepan with the lemon zest and juice, and then pour the juices gradually into the flour mixture, mixing as you pour, to a soft dough. Take pieces of the dough, press them out between the palms of your hands into fairly thin pieces and lay them on top of the apricots so that the whole tart is covered. Patch any holes with little bits of pastry and press the pastry

down into the dish at the edges. Refrigerate the tart for at least 30 minutes.

To cook, preheat the oven to Gas Mark 7/220°C/425°F. Pierce four holes in the pastry to allow the steam to escape. Cook in the centre of the oven for 25 minutes or until the pastry has browned. Turn down the heat to Gas Mark 2/150°C/300°F and continue cooking for another 30 minutes. Turn off the heat but leave the tart in the oven for about 15 minutes.

While still warm, loosen the edges of the tart with a knife, put a large serving plate on top of the flan dish and turn the tart upside down to unmould, revealing the apricots. Brush the warmed honey all over the apricots and serve the tart warm, if possible, and on its own or with fresh cream.
Serves 6

CLEAR RHUBARB AND RED WINE JELLY FLAVOURED WITH GINGER

Even people who say they don't like rhubarb welcome this with enthusiasm after a large meal. In season, fresh elderflowers add a wonderfully scented flavour to the jelly and look pretty as a decoration.

250g (8oz) rhubarb
2.5cm (1-inch) piece of fresh root
*   ginger*
3 elderflower heads (optional)
50g (2oz) granulated sugar
4 tablespoons lemon juice
Juice of 1 orange
450ml (¾ pint) red wine
2 tablespoons water
3 teaspoons gelatine powder or
*   3 tablespoons agar-agar flakes*

Cut the rhubarb and ginger up into rough pieces and place in a large saucepan. Wash the elderflower heads, if using, before pulling off the flowers and adding them to the saucepan together with the sugar. Using a fine sieve, strain the lemon and orange juice

into the mixture, followed by the red wine. Put the pan over the heat, bring the mixture to the boil and then allow it to simmer gently for about 15 minutes or until the rhubarb is completely mushy. Remove the pan from the heat and strain the liquid into a mixing bowl. Then strain the liquid back through the finest strainer into another bowl or clean saucepan.

Put the water into a separate saucepan, bring it up to boiling and then remove the pan from the heat. Then sprinkle the gelatine powder or agar-agar flakes into the water, following the packet instructions to ensure it dissolves thoroughly. Stir the gelatine mixture into the strained rhubarb and wine liquid. Pour the mixture into a 1.25-litre (2¼-pint) metal jelly mould or into individual moulds and leave until cold. Then put it in the refrigerator to set.

Before serving, dip the mould briefly in hot water and turn the jelly out on to a serving plate, giving it a shake against the plate to release it.
TO SERVE Decorate the jelly with

sprigs of elderflower or rose petals, or whatever edible flowers are available.
Serves 4

▲ *Clear rhubarb and red wine jelly flavoured with ginger*

◄ *Honey-glazed fresh apricot tart*

135

VANISHING SOUFFLÉ
WITH CHOCOLATE BRANDY CUSTARD

This is a steamed, sweetened egg white soufflé which literally does vanish in your mouth. Pure white, it is served with a chocolate brandy custard made from the egg yolks.

4 large eggs (size 1), separated
50g (2oz) plus 1 tablespoon caster sugar
1 tablespoon brandy
150ml (¼ pint) double cream
50g (2oz) plain chocolate, grated

In a clean bowl, whisk the egg whites until thick, then whisk in 50g (2oz) of the caster sugar. Continue whisking until the mixture stands in stiff peaks. Spoon the egg white into a soufflé dish; then put the dish into a large, deep saucepan filled with hot water (the pudding will rise spectacularly) so that the hot water comes three-quarters of the way up the sides of the dish. Cover the saucepan and cook over the lowest heat (the water must not even simmer) for 1½ hours.

Meanwhile make the sauce. Whisk the egg yolks in a bowl with the remaining tablespoon of caster sugar and the brandy. Place the cream in a pouring saucepan and bring it to a rolling boil, then pour it immediately on to the egg yolks, whisking swiftly all the time. Whisk in the grated chocolate thoroughly, then leave the custard to cool. Once it has cooled down, chill the custard in the refrigerator.

When the pudding is ready, remove the soufflé dish from the pan, allow it to cool and then chill the soufflé in the refrigerator. During chilling, it may shrink quite a lot.
TO SERVE On individual plates, pour a pool of custard. Using a large serving spoon, take up a heaped spoonful of the soufflé and place on the pool of custard.
Serves 5–6

SHARP LEMON SOUFFLÉ
ON A CHOCOLATE SHORTBREAD BASE

This is a wonderfully light and frothy hot soufflé. People often think it is impractical to make a soufflé for the end of the meal but as this pudding is made in stages, almost all of it can be done well in advance. All you have left to do at the end is fold in the egg whites just before cooking. Since the actual cooking takes approximately one hour, this means that the soufflé will be ready just about the time you finish the first part of the meal. The contrast between the sharpness of the lemon and richness of the chocolate is superb.

FOR THE CHOCOLATE SHORTBREAD:
150g (5oz) plain flour
25g (1oz) cocoa powder
½ teaspoon salt
3 heaped tablespoons caster sugar
150g (5oz) soft butter
FOR THE SOUFFLÉ:
4 large eggs (size 1)
75g (3oz) caster sugar
150ml (¼ pint) freshly squeezed lemon juice (approximately 3–4 lemons)
Finely grated zest of 2 lemons
Salt

◄ *Vanishing soufflé with chocolate brandy custard*

To make the shortbread, preheat the oven to Gas Mark 6/200°C/400°F. Butter a 23cm (9-inch) china flan dish. Sift the flour, cocoa, salt and sugar together into a bowl. Work the butter into the flour mixture with your fingertips. Then, using floured hands, gather it together and press the dough lightly but evenly over the bottom of the flan dish. Prick the base of the shortbread all over with a fork and refrigerate it for at least 20 minutes. Cook the shortbread on the centre shelf of the oven, for 15–20 minutes. Allow the shortbread base to cool.

While the shortbread is cooking, begin to make the soufflé. Separate the eggs. Put the egg yolks into the top of a double saucepan or a bowl set over a pan of hot water. Put the whites into a large whisking bowl. Stir the sugar into the egg yolks and then, a little at a time, add the lemon juice. Put the saucepan over a medium heat and stir all the time until it has thickened to make a lemon custard which coats the back of the spoon. Stir in the grated zest and leave the custard to cool.

Preheat the oven to Gas Mark 2/150°C/300°F. Add a pinch of salt to the egg whites and whisk the whites until they hold soft peaks. Then, using a metal spoon, lightly fold the cooled lemon custard into the egg whites. Pile the mixture on top of the base. Cook the soufflé towards the top of the oven for 50 to 60 minutes until browned.
TO SERVE Serve the soufflé with soft fruit, cream or crème fraîche, and, in season, with a bowl of fresh raspberries.
Serves 6

▲ *Sharp lemon soufflé on a chocolate shortbread base*

CARROT TART WITH CANDIED CARROT TOPPING

This foolproof recipe is based on the description of a tart I once read in a Victorian book. The glossy orange top gives it a most striking appearance.

FOR THE PASTRY:
150g (5oz) plain flour
½ teaspoon salt
50g (2oz) icing sugar
1 egg
75g (3oz) soft butter
FOR THE FILLING:
50g (2oz) butter
2 eggs
2 egg yolks
250ml (8 fl oz) single cream or milk
125g (4oz) caster sugar
50g (2oz) fresh white breadcrumbs
Finely grated zest of 1 lemon
75g (3oz) grated carrot
½ whole nutmeg, grated
FOR THE TOPPING:
250g (8oz) carrots
175g (6oz) white granulated sugar
4 tablespoons lemon juice
4 tablespoons water

Make the pastry in advance. Sift the flour, salt and icing sugar into a mixing bowl. Make a well in the centre. Whisk the egg lightly with a fork and drop it in. Then add the butter and work the mixture together with your hands until it is well blended, about 1–2 minutes. Dust your hands with flour and knead the dough lightly with the palms of your hands until you have a smooth ball of dough. Wrap the dough in clingfilm and chill for at least one hour.

To make the filling, melt the butter and leave it to cool slightly. In a mixing bowl, whisk together the eggs, egg yolks, melted butter, cream and the caster sugar. Stir in the breadcrumbs, lemon zest, grated carrot and nutmeg.

Set the oven to preheat at Gas Mark 4/180°C/350°F, and butter a 25–26cm (10–10½-inch) loose-bottomed fluted flan tin. Roll out the chilled pastry on a well-floured surface into a circle a little bigger than the flan tin. Line the tin with the pastry, turning the slightly overlapping edges in again to make a neat thick edge. Prick the base of the pastry case all over with a fork. Pour the prepared filling into the pastry case. Bake the tart in the centre of the oven for 45–50 minutes or until the filling is golden and has risen slightly.

Finally, to make the topping, peel and slice the carrots into roughly 5cm (2-inch) long julienne strips (use the special blade of the food processor for this if you have one). Put the strips into a saucepan with the sugar, lemon juice and water over a medium heat. Stir to dissolve the sugar, then increase the heat and boil briskly for about five minutes or until a blob of syrup sets on a cold saucer. Remove the pan from the heat and allow the topping to cool slightly before spreading it all over the top of the tart. Serve the tart either warm or at room temperature. Before serving, put the tin on a jam jar and carefully push the sides down. Using a wide spatula, carefully ease the tart off the base on to a large flat serving plate.
Serves 8

WHITE PEAR CAKE

This cake has a tender white crumb and is topped with pears spiced with cinnamon. It can be served warm with cream or yogurt as a pudding or eaten cold as a special teatime treat. I have also made an equally delicious version using apples instead of pears.

50g (2oz) soft butter
3 tablespoons soft light brown sugar
Finely grated zest of 2 lemons
2 teaspoons ground cinnamon
500g (1lb) firm pears
175g (6oz) plain flour
2 teaspoons baking powder
½ teaspoon salt
6 tablespoons sunflower oil
8 tablespoons lemon juice
6 tablespoons milk
2 large egg whites (size 1)
Pinch of cream of tartar
175g (6oz) caster sugar

◄ *Carrot tart with candied carrot topping*

Spread the butter thickly over the bottom and rather more thinly up the sides of a 23cm (9-inch) cake tin. Mix together the brown sugar, lemon zest and cinnamon. Spread two-thirds of this mixture over the butter on the base of the tin. Peel and slice the pears thinly, and overlap on top of the sugar. Sprinkle the remaining sugar on top. Set the oven to preheat at Gas Mark 4/180°C/350°F.

Sift the flour, baking powder and salt into a bowl. Pour in the oil. Strain in the lemon juice, add the milk and beat until you have a thick, smooth batter. In a separate bowl, whisk the egg whites until foamy. Add the cream of tartar and whisk again until the mixture is stiff but not breaking up. Gradually whisk in the caster sugar. Using a metal spoon, fold the mixture into the batter and then pour it on top of the pears in the tin. Cook the cake on the centre shelf of the oven for 50–60 minutes. Leave the cake to cool in the tin for about 10 minutes; then turn the cake out, upside-down, on to a serving plate.

▲ *White pear cake*

ROSE PETAL SORBET WITH CRYSTALLIZED PETALS

The petals of heavily scented roses have a unique flavour for which I developed a passion during my childhood in the Middle East. Later on I was reacquainted with it in the delectable rose petal jams of Turkey, and in many Indian sweets. After a large meal, this romantic sorbet is the perfect light and reviving finale. Serve it with a bowl of Greek yogurt.

FOR THE SORBET:
Petals of 4 heavily scented red roses
1.2 litres (2 pints) water
500g (1lb) caster sugar
4 tablespoons lemon juice
½–1 tablespoon rose water
2 large egg whites (size 1)
¼ teaspoon salt
FOR THE CRYSTALLIZED PETALS:
1 large egg white (size 1)
Petals of 1 large heavily scented red rose
Caster sugar

To make the sorbet, wash the rose petals and put them in a saucepan with the water. Bring the water to the boil, cover the pan and simmer gently for 10 minutes. Remove the pan from the heat and strain the water into another saucepan, reserving the petals. Add the caster sugar to the strained water and put the pan over a low heat, stirring until the sugar has completely dissolved. Then bring to the boil and boil fiercely, without stirring, for three minutes. Remove from the heat and stir in the lemon juice, and the extra rose water to taste. Then stir in the reserved rose petals and leave until cold.

When the mixture is cold pour it into a mixing bowl and put it in the freezer. When the sorbet is half-frozen, take it out and break it up to a mush with a fork. In a bowl, whisk the egg whites with the salt until they stand in soft peaks and fold them gently but thoroughly into the rose petal sorbet with a metal spoon. Transfer the sorbet

to a pretty serving bowl – glass looks best – and put it back in the freezer.

Now make the crystallized rose petals. Put a piece of greaseproof paper on a large baking sheet. Whisk the egg white until stiff but not breaking up. Paint each rose petal lightly with egg white, then dip it in the bowl of caster sugar, shaking off the excess. Lay the coated petals on the greaseproof paper. Put them in a warm dry place, such as the airing cupboard, for 1–1½ hours or until the petals are quite dry and crisp. Then carefully peel the petals off the paper. If you are not going to eat the sorbet for several hours, or until the next day, keep the petals in an air-tight container – they must be kept absolutely dry.

Shortly before serving, scatter a few crystallized petals on the sorbet. Put the remaining crystallized petals into a pretty bowl on the table for your guests to scatter on to their individual serving.
Serves 6

GODDESS OF PUDDINGS

Along with bread and butter pudding, queen of puddings is a justly famous English classic and the epitome of comfort food. This variation, which is made with citrus zest and marmalade instead of the red jam traditionally used in queen of puddings, is to me even better than the original version. This pudding can be served either hot or cold, with or without cream, depending on your taste and the occasion.

75g (3oz) fresh white breadcrumbs
600ml (1 pint) milk
Finely grated zest of 2 oranges
Juice and finely grated zest of 1 lemon
50g (2oz) butter
3 large eggs (size 1), separated
125g (4oz) golden caster sugar
4 rounded tablespoons Seville orange marmalade
¼ teaspoon salt

◀ *Rose petal sorbet with crystallized petals*

Set the oven to preheat at Gas Mark 4/180°C/350°F. Butter an oval or rectangular ovenproof dish. Spread the breadcrumbs over the bottom of the dish. Put the milk into a saucepan and add the finely grated zest of one orange and the lemon. Add the butter and stir over a low heat until the butter has melted and the mixture is just warm. Lightly whisk together the egg yolks and 75g (3oz) of the caster sugar. Then gradually stir in the heated milk and butter and pour over the breadcrumbs. Bake the custard in the centre of the oven for about 25 minutes or until the custard has set to a light touch in the centre. Then remove the custard from the oven. Mix the lemon juice into the marmalade and spread the marmalade over the top. In a clean bowl, whisk the egg whites with the salt until they stand in soft peaks. Using a metal spoon, fold the remaining sugar and the finely grated zest of the remaining orange into the egg whites. Pile this meringue

over the marmalade and sprinkle a very little extra caster sugar over the top. Return the pudding to the oven for 10–15 minutes or until golden brown.
Serves 6

▲ *Goddess of puddings*

CHOCOLATE CAKE WITH VANILLA AND CINNAMON

A very chocolaty cake with a delicate crumb, this is equally good as a pudding with soft fruit or cream.

175g (6oz) plain chocolate
125g (4oz) soft butter
150g (5oz) caster sugar
3 teaspoons vanilla essence
2 teaspoons ground cinnamon
4 large eggs (size 1), separated
2 tablespoons self-raising flour
1 tablespoon cocoa powder
Pinch of salt
Icing sugar, to decorate

Set the oven to preheat at Gas Mark 4/180°C/350°F . Butter a deep 17–18cm (6½–7-inch) cake tin. Line the base with buttered baking parchment. Dust the tin with flour. Place the chocolate in a bowl set over a pan of very hot but not boiling water, stirring until the chocolate has melted. Whisk together the butter and sugar until soft and fluffy. Then whisk in the chocolate, the vanilla and cinnamon and the egg yolks. Sift the flour and cocoa on to the mixture and lightly whisk in.

Whisk the egg whites with the salt until they hold soft peaks, and fold into the chocolate mixture. Turn into the prepared tin and cook in the centre of the oven for about 40 minutes, or until the cake has risen and a crust has formed on top. Don't pierce to test it.

Leave the cake in the tin for 10 minutes, then invert it on to a cake rack and remove the paper. Finally, turn the cake right side up (it may sink a little) and sieve or sprinkle icing sugar over the top. Transfer the cake on to a serving plate.

SQUIDGY PRUNE, PECAN, CITRUS AND HONEY CAKE

This uses the old-fashioned method of boiling the ingredients before baking.

175g (6oz) butter
175g (6oz) soft brown sugar
300ml (½ pint) water
250g (8oz) stoned prunes, chopped
50g (2oz) stem ginger, chopped
Coarsely grated zest and juice of
*   1 orange and 1 lemon*
175g (6oz) pecan pieces
250g (8oz) plain flour
1 teaspoon bicarbonate of soda
1 teaspoon ground cinnamon
2 large eggs
1 tablespoon honey
Half pecans, to decorate

Grease a deep 15–18cm (6–7-inch) cake tin and line the bottom with baking parchment. In a saucepan, dissolve the butter and sugar in the water. Place the prunes, ginger, orange and lemon zest and nuts into the saucepan. Bring to the boil, cover, and simmer gently for 10–15 minutes. Leave to cool. Set the oven to preheat at Gas Mark 4/180°C/350°F . Sift the flour and bicarbonate of soda into a mixing bowl and add the cinnamon; then stir in the cool fruit mixture with a wooden spoon. In a separate bowl, whisk the eggs until frothy and mix them thoroughly into the fruit mixture. Pour the cake mixture into the prepared

tin, place half pecans all over the top and bake in the centre of the oven for about 1¼ hours, or until a knife inserted in the centre comes out clean.

Using a fine skewer, pierce the warm cake all over through to the bottom. Put the honey into a small saucepan and strain in the orange and lemon juice. Stir to dissolve the honey over a medium heat, then allow the mixture to bubble fiercely for two minutes. Spoon this syrup slowly over the cake, allowing it to absorb into the skewer holes. Leave the cake to cool in the tin, then loosen the sides of the cake with a knife and turn it out. Wrap the cake in clingfilm until ready to eat.

CITRUS-DRENCHED CAKE

250g (8oz) butter
250g (8oz) soft light brown sugar
4 large eggs (size 1)
Finely grated zest and juice of 2–3
*   lemons*
50g (2oz) ground almonds
175g (6oz) self-raising flour
2 teaspoons baking powder
½ teaspoon salt
3 tablespoons fresh orange juice
50g (2oz) caster sugar

◀ *Chocolate cake with vanilla pod and cinnamon; squidgy prune, pecan, citrus and honey cake; citrus-drenched cake*

Set the oven to preheat at Gas Mark 4/180°C/350°F. Butter a 19cm (7½-inch) cake tin and line it with buttered baking parchment. Dust the tin with flour. In a large bowl, whisk the butter until soft and then whisk in the brown sugar until fluffy. Thoroughly whisk in one egg at a time.Whisk in the lemon zest and then stir in the almonds. In a separate bowl, sift together the flour, baking powder and salt and stir this into the egg mixture. Spoon this mixture into the tin and level the top. Cook in the centre of the oven for 1¼–1½ hours or until the cake is

springy, and a knife inserted in the middle comes out clean. If it browns too much, cover loosely with foil.

Strain the lemon juice into a saucepan. Add the orange juice and the caster sugar and stir over a low heat to dissolve the sugar. Then boil fiercely without stirring for two minutes. Pierce the cake, still in its tin, right through all over with a skewer and spoon the citrus syrup on to it very gradually, allowing the juices to seep into the holes. Leave the cake in the tin until almost cold, then loosen the sides with a knife and turn the cake out.

BREADS, BISCUITS & PRESERVES

When putting together a cookery book, there are always odds and ends which don't fit into any of the chapter categories. But to me, they are often things which are so delicious or full of good memories that I just have to put them in somewhere; this is certainly true of my ambrosial apricot jam flavoured with elderflowers. And there is still something particularly special about bread-making. Now that we have easy blend yeast, which makes bread-making so much less laborious than it used to be, it is tempting to try out all sorts of different breads with added ingredients; they can really be the making of a

light lunch or picnic. Basic bread recipes can be adapted in many different ways. Perhaps the breads I have produced will inspire you to try out variations of your own. It is, I find, almost impossible to make the same bread twice. So many exciting and delicious possibilities are offered by the huge range of herbs and spices available nowadays, not to mention cheeses and olives and all the other things you can find on modern delicatessen counters. Children seem to love making bread, biscuits and snacks. So I hope that this final little medley will have something to attract cooks of all ages.

KEN BUGGY'S IRISH SODA BREAD

Ken Buggy makes everyone welcome at his charming B & B in Kinsale, Co. Cork. Every morning at breakfast his warm, freshly baked soda bread is on the table. This is his own recipe which I have used ever since I spent a happy few days there. In Ireland you can get coarser ground wholemeal flour than elsewhere, which is why in this recipe I grind some wheat grains to achieve the true Irish effect. Soda bread must be eaten very fresh, preferably warm, but since it takes only five minutes to make and 30 minutes to cook, this is easily possible. Ken Buggy stresses that not only should this dough not be kneaded but it should be handled as lightly and briefly as possible when you are gathering it up into a rather rough-looking round loaf.

◀ *Ken Buggy's Irish soda bread*

125g (4oz) wholewheat grain
125g (4oz) stoneground wholemeal flour
375g (12oz) strong white flour
2–3 teaspoons crushed sea salt
2 tablespoons bran
1 rounded teaspoon bicarbonate of soda
450–600ml (¾–1 pint) buttermilk

Set the oven to preheat at Gas Mark 8/230°C/450°F. Put the wheat grains into an electric coffee grinder and whizz just until coarsely ground and still bitty. Put these grains into a large mixing bowl and add the stoneground wholemeal flour, strong white flour, sea salt, bran and the bicarbonate of soda. Using a wooden spoon, mix all these dry ingredients together well.

Then, using a wooden spoon, gradually and lightly stir in the

buttermilk until you have a soft dough which just about sticks together enough to leave the side of the mixing bowl as you stir. Handling the dough very lightly, quickly gather the dough up to form a rough, round ball. Do not knead it at all.

Thoroughly flour a baking sheet. Put the ball of dough on to the baking sheet and, using a large sharp knife, cut a deep cross almost, but not completely, through the dough.

Place the loaf on a shelf just above the centre of the preheated oven and bake for about 30 minutes. When the bread is ready, it should sound hollow when you tap the underside. Then turn the loaf upside down and put it back in the oven for a further 2–3 minutes just to firm up the crust on the base of the loaf. Eat the loaf while it is still warm, if possible, or at least freshly baked.

GREEK SALAD BREAD

This bread, served while it is still warm (or reheated) with a green salad, is a meal in itself.

9 tablespoons olive oil
3 medium onions, chopped finely
750g (1½lb) strong plain white flour
2 rounded teaspoons crushed sea salt
3 rounded teaspoons dried oregano
2 teaspoons whole coriander seeds
1 rounded teaspoon green peppercorns
150g (5oz) feta cheese, cubed roughly
4 tomatoes, chopped
50g (2oz) stoned black olives, halved
2 envelopes easy blend yeast

Put three tablespoons of the olive oil in a large frying pan over a medium high heat. Fry the chopped onion until soft and well browned, stirring often. Then turn the onion into a bowl to cool slightly. Put the white flour into a large bowl and stir in the sea salt, oregano, coriander seeds and peppercorns. Add the feta cheese, tomatoes, olives and all but a small spoonful of the onion to the mixture. Put the remaining oil into a measuring jug and bring up the liquid to 450ml (¾ pint) with warm water. Stir the liquid gradually into the bread mixture. Mix in the yeast. Then, using floured hands, gather up the dough and form it into two balls. Generously oil two 18–20cm (7–8-inch) cake tins. Place one ball of dough in each tin and cut a deep cross in each. Sprinkle the dough with the reserved onions. Put the tins inside a large plastic bin liner, puffing the bag up and turning it under the tins to trap the air. Leave the dough at room temperature for about two hours until it is well risen.

Bake the loaves, side by side if possible, on the centre shelf of a preheated oven, Gas Mark 8/230°C/450°F, for 20 minutes. Then turn down the heat to Gas Mark 6/200°C/400°F, and cook the loaves for another 20 minutes, or until the bread sounds hollow when tapped on the underside. Turn the loaves out on to a rack to cool slightly and eat warm. This bread does not need to be buttered unless you prefer it.

ANGLO-SYRIAN BREAD

As a child in Damascus, I remember the flat, unleavened bread being the best I have ever tasted. However, in a conventional loaf, I can incorporate many of the other ingredients and combinations which I started to love in those Middle Eastern days. This loaf, full of nuts, seeds and spices is a wonderful accompaniment to a salad lunch. Easy blend dried yeast makes bread-making simple enough even for inexperienced cooks. Shelled pistachio nuts are an excellent alternative to the walnuts.

1 large onion, chopped
50g (2oz) pine kernels
500g (1lb) strong plain white flour
1 tablespoon crushed sea salt
2 teaspoons cumin seeds
2 teaspoons coriander seeds, crushed roughly
75g (3oz) sesame seeds
75g (3oz) walnut pieces, ground roughly
Generous handful of mint leaves, chopped roughly
4 tablespoons extra virgin olive oil
1 envelope easy blend yeast
300ml (½ pint) water

Smear a 25 x 5cm (10 x 2-inch) circular earthenware dish or cake tin with olive oil. Put the chopped onion into a dry frying pan over a high heat and stir just to darken the pieces of onion. Then add all but one tablespoon of the pine kernels. Toss for a minute just until the kernels are browned and remove the pan from the heat. Put the flour and sea salt into a mixing bowl and stir together. Then stir in the cumin and coriander seeds, all but two teaspoons of the sesame seeds, the walnut pieces and the fried onion and pine kernels. Stir the chopped mint into the mixture. Stir in the olive oil, mix in the yeast and then gradually add the water, just until the mixture sticks together. Then gather up and knead the dough lightly on a floured surface for about five minutes. Put the dough into the oiled dish or tin. Cut a deep star in the top and scatter with the reserved unbrowned pine kernels and sesame seeds. Cover the dish or tin with a large plastic bag tucked in under the dish, trapping plenty of air and ballooning up above the dough. Leave the dish at room temperature for about two hours or until the dough has doubled in size.

Remove the plastic and place the loaf on the centre shelf of a preheated oven, Gas Mark 8/230°C/450°F, for 20 minutes; then turn down the heat to Gas Mark 6/200°C/400°F and leave the bread to bake for a further 20 minutes. Turn the loaf out of the dish and leave it to cool on a rack.

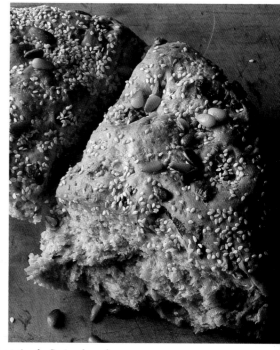

◀ *Greek salad bread*

▲ *Anglo-Syrian bread*

147

ANCHOVY, GARLIC AND PARSLEY STICKS

If you keep puff pastry in your freezer, and anchovies in the store cupboard, you can make these appetizing little sticks on the spur of the moment. They go ideally with drinks before a meal.

50g (2oz) can of anchovy fillets
1 large garlic clove
Handful of parsley, trimmed
250g (8oz) puff pastry
1 egg yolk
Black pepper
Grated Parmesan cheese, to
  sprinkle

Set the oven to preheat at Gas Mark 6/200°C/400°F. Empty the anchovy fillets, together with their oil, into the bowl of a food processor. Add the garlic and parsley and plenty of black pepper and whizz as finely as possible.

Divide the pastry in half. Roll out both halves on a flat surface into two rectangles not more than 3mm (⅛-inch) thick. Spread the anchovy mixture evenly over one rectangle, and then place the other rectangle on top and press down lightly all over.

Using a sharp knife, cut the pastry into sticks about 6 x 2cm (2 x ¾-inch) long. Grease a large baking sheet and arrange the sticks on it. Brush the sticks with egg yolk and sprinkle lightly with the Parmesan cheese.

Place the sticks on a shelf just above the centre of the oven and bake for about 10–15 minutes until the sticks have puffed up and are golden brown. *TO SERVE* If possible, serve the sticks warm — you can either keep them warm in a low oven or simply re-heat them when you are ready.
Makes about 24 sticks

ORANGE AND ROSEMARY FINGER BISCUITS

This is the most convenient way of being able to produce homemade freshly baked biscuits. You make up the dough, form it into a long roll and keep it in the freezer so that every time you want some biscuits, you simply slice as many as you need off the roll and put them straight into the oven on a baking tray. They cook in 10 minutes and keep really well in an airtight container.

1 x 8cm (3-inch) sprig of fresh
  rosemary
125g (4oz) butter
200g (7oz) caster sugar
1 large egg
Finely grated zest of 1 large orange
250g (8oz) plain flour
2 teaspoons baking powder
½ teaspoon salt

Pull the rosemary spikes off their stem and chop them finely. Whisk the butter and sugar together until pale and light. Beat the egg lightly with a fork and whisk it into the butter and sugar thoroughly, a little at a time.

Then stir in the chopped rosemary and grated orange zest. Sift the flour with the baking powder and salt into a bowl. Stir the flour into the butter mixture. Flour your hands and shape the dough into a long, rather flat roll. If you find the dough is too soft to shape easily, refrigerate it briefly until it becomes firmer. Wrap the roll up in clingfilm and lay it on a flat surface in the freezer.

Whenever you want the biscuits, have a large ungreased baking sheet ready and preheat oven to Gas Mark 5/190°C/375°F. Take the frozen roll of dough from the freezer, and using a sharp knife, slice off the biscuits as thinly as you can.

Place the biscuits on the baking sheet a little apart, as they expand during cooking. Place the baking sheet in the centre of the preheated oven, and bake the biscuits for 7–9 minutes until they are a pale golden colour.

Immediately, while they are still hot, ease the biscuits off the tray with a palette knife and put them on a rack to cool. If you want curved biscuits, drape them over a rolling pin or any other cylindrical object and leave to cool. *TO SERVE* These light and buttery biscuits are perfect for tea parties or with ice creams or fruity puddings.
Makes about 50 biscuits

HIGHLAND OATCAKES

I first tasted these in the Outer Hebrides off the north-west coast of Scotland. We had them every day, either simply spread with butter or with locally made honey. They are perfect with cheese.

125g (4oz) medium oatmeal
½ teaspoon salt
Generous pinch of bicarbonate of
  soda
4 tablespoons water
15g (½ oz) butter

Set the oven to preheat at Gas Mark 5/190°C/375°F. Mix together the oatmeal, salt and bicarbonate of soda in a bowl. Bring the water to the boil in a small saucepan. Add the butter and stir until melted. Pour the liquid into the oat mixture and stir thoroughly until you have a fairly moist dough. Sprinkle a baking sheet thinly with oatmeal. Form the dough into a ball and put it into the centre of the baking sheet. Using the palm of your hands, press the dough into a rough 20cm (8-inch) circle. Press along the edge to neaten it slightly. Using a sharp knife, score the circle almost through each way into eight triangular slices. Cook in the centre of the oven for 20–25 minutes. Leave the oatcakes on a rack to cool.
Makes 8 cakes

▶ *Anchovy, garlic and parsley sticks; orange and rosemary finger biscuits; Highland oatcakes*

TOMATO, HERB, PARMESAN AND GARLIC BREAD WITH OLIVE OIL

I have made many versions of this Italian-style bread, but this one, without olives, has been the most popular of all. Served warm, it makes a light lunch with cheese and salad.

375g (12oz) strong or unbleached plain white flour
2 level tablespoons crushed sea salt
75g (3oz) whole Parmesan
2 large sprigs of fresh rosemary
10–12 basil leaves
12–15 sage leaves
10–12 sun-dried tomatoes, sliced thinly
2 large garlic cloves, chopped finely
5 tablespoons extra virgin olive oil
1 envelope easy blend yeast
Water

Oil a large pizza tin or baking sheet. Put the flour into a large bowl and stir in all but two teaspoons of the sea salt. Pare off a little Parmesan with a potato peeler for decoration, and grate the remainder. Chop one sprig of rosemary. Thinly slice the basil and all but two of the sage leaves. Add the grated Parmesan, chopped rosemary, sliced basil and sage, tomatoes and garlic to the flour. Stir with a wooden spoon, then stir in three tablespoons of the oil. Mix in the yeast, then add enough water to form a slightly sticky, soft dough. Knead on a very lightly floured surface for about five minutes until smooth and elastic.

Form the dough into a ball, then press it out with your hand into a very rough circle about 1–2cm (½–¾ inch) thick and 25cm (10 inches) in diameter. Transfer the dough to the oiled sheet and, using a wooden salad fork, prick the surface deeply all over.

Put the tin inside a large plastic bag and fold the bag in under the tin, trapping plenty of air so that it is puffed up. Leave at room temperature for about two hours until the dough has doubled in thickness.

Remove the bag and trickle over the remaining oil, spreading it lightly and letting it sit in any dips. Sprinkle on the reserved Parmesan, sage and sea salt and whole rosemary. Bake in the centre of a preheated oven, Gas Mark 7/220°C/425°F for about 20 minutes or until the top is dark golden brown.

AROMATIC VEGETABLE PASTIES WITH YOGURT PASTRY

These pasties are especially good for picnics. The pastry is light and crispy and the pasties can be eaten cold (but not chilled), although they are nicest warm. Use red onions if available.

FOR THE FILLING:
15g (½oz) butter
2 tablespoons olive oil
250g (8oz) onions, chopped finely
1 garlic clove, chopped finely
175g (6oz) potatoes, cut in small cubes
2 teaspoons ground coriander
1 teaspoon ground cumin
125g (4oz) frozen petits pois
Handful of fresh mint leaves, chopped finely
Salt and black pepper
FOR THE PASTRY:
125g (4oz) butter
1 tablespoon olive oil
1 small egg (size 3)
150ml (¼ pint) natural yogurt
300g (10oz) plain flour
¼ teaspoon bicarbonate of soda
1 teaspoon salt
1 egg yolk

To make the filling, melt the butter and oil in a large frying pan over a medium heat. Add the onions and garlic, and cook for a few minutes, stirring occasionally until the onions begin to soften. Add the potatoes and cook for 5–7 minutes, stirring occasionally, until they are just soft. Stir in the spices and cook for one minute; then remove from the heat. Add the petits pois. Turn the mixture into a bowl and season it well. Stir in the mint. Leave the mixture on one side until cold.

Lightly grease a large baking sheet and preheat the oven to Gas Mark 6/200°C/400°F. To make the pastry, melt the butter and then leave it to cool. Whisk together the olive oil and egg, stir in the yogurt, then, using a wooden spoon, stir the melted butter into the yogurt mixture, a little at a time, until smoothly mixed. Sift the flour, bicarbonate of soda and salt together. Gradually stir the flour into the yogurt mixture to form a soft dough. Turn out on to a lightly floured surface and knead gently for a few minutes. Then roll the dough out to about 5mm (¼ inch) thick. Using the rim of a glass about 10cm (4 inches) in diameter, cut out circles from the pastry. Spoon about two teaspoons of the filling on to one side of each circle. Fold the pastry over to form a semi-circular pasty. Press the edges to seal. Place on the baking sheet and brush with egg yolk. Bake for about 20 minutes or until the pasties are golden
Makes 6

▲ *Aromatic vegetable pasties with yogurt pastry*

◄ *Tomato, herb, Parmesan and garlic bread with olive oil*

AMBROSIAL APRICOT JAM

This jam is even better flavoured with elderflowers. Pull off the tiny flowers and stir them into the apricots instead of the mint. The elderflower version is the best jam I have ever made.

1.75kg (4lbs) ripe apricots
300ml (½ pint) freshly squeezed
  orange juice
4 tablespoons lemon juice
1.75kg (4lbs) sugar with pectin
15g (½oz) unsalted butter
6 teaspoons chopped fresh mint or
  4–5 elderflower heads
3–5 tablespoons apricot brandy
  (optional)

Wash out the jam jars and put them on a baking sheet in a very low oven to sterilize them. Halve the apricots and remove but reserve the stones. Using a nut cracker, open about half or more of the stones and take out the kernel. Boil the kernels in a small saucepan of water for one minute, then drain.

Now put the kernels and apricot halves into a preserving pan. Place the orange juice in a measuring jug, add the lemon juice and bring the total liquid quantity up to 450ml (¾ pint) with water. Add this liquid to the apricots. Put the preserving pan over the heat, bring to the boil and simmer the liquid for 10–15 minutes, or until the apricots are soft but not mushy.

Remove the pan from the heat and add the sugar, stirring until it dissolves. Then stir in the butter. Next, stir in the chopped mint. Return the pan to the heat, bring the jam to the boil and boil rapidly for 4–5 minutes. If you have a sugar thermometer, it will tell you when setting point is reached; otherwise, put a drop of jam on a cold saucer and place it in the freezing compartment of the refrigerator for one minute to see if it sets — you don't want the jam to be too set. Remove any scum from the top of the mixture with a spoon. Add the apricot brandy, if using, and leave the jam for 15 minutes before potting. Then remove the tray of warm jars from the oven and ladle the jam into them. Cover the tops of the jars with wax discs before sealing with a lid or cellophane. Leave to cool.
Makes about 6 x 500g (1lb) jars

AUBERGINE, APRICOT AND TOMATO CHUTNEY

125g (4oz) dried apricots, chopped
450ml (¾ pint) freshly squeezed
  orange juice
2 aubergines
8 large garlic cloves, chopped finely
8cm (3-inch) piece of fresh root
  ginger, chopped finely
8 cardamom pods, crushed roughly
2 teaspoons cumin seeds
300ml (½ pint) cider vinegar
3 tablespoons sherry vinegar
375g (12oz) light muscovado sugar
2 x 400g (13oz) cans of chopped
  tomatoes
2 teaspoons salt
½ teaspoon chilli powder

Wash out four 1lb preserving jars and place them on a baking sheet in a very low oven to sterilize them.

Put the apricots into a bowl with the orange juice. Leave the apricots to soak for about one hour. Bring a saucepan of water to the boil, then cut the aubergines into 2.5cm (1-inch) cubes and drop the cubes into the boiling water. Boil the aubergines for five minutes and then drain.

Put the soaked apricots and their juice, the aubergine, garlic and ginger, cardamom pods and cumin seeds into a large, heavy saucepan. Pour in both vinegars and stir in the sugar and the tomatoes. Add two teaspoons of salt. Bring the mixture to the boil, then lower the heat and simmer gently in the open pan for 1½ to 1¾ hours, stirring occasionally at first and more often as the mixture thickens. Finally, season to taste with chilli powder and more salt if necessary. Then spoon the chutney immediately into the sterilized jars. Seal the jars at once with cellophane or vacuum lids.
TO SERVE This chutney is mild, but has an aromatic, sweet and sour taste. Serve it with bread and cheese, with spicy dishes and with scrambled eggs.
Makes about 1.75kg (4lbs)

SWEET PICKLED SHALLOTS

500g (1lb) shallots, peeled
4 tablespoons wine vinegar
300ml (½ pint) extra virgin olive oil
  (approximately)
1 tablespoon clear honey
2 dried red chillies (optional)
Sea salt and black pepper

◄ *Ambrosial apricot jam; aubergine, apricot and tomato chutney; sweet pickled shallots*

Put the whole shallots into a small saucepan with the vinegar and enough water to cover. Bring to the boil, then cover the pan and simmer gently for 30–45 minutes or until the shallots are soft right through. Then drain them and toss them in the oil. Place the shallots on a baking tray and put them under a fairly hot grill for a few minutes, turning them once or twice, until they are dark brown to black in patches. Put them into a bowl with the honey and a sprinkling of sea salt and pepper. Mix together gently. Pack the shallots into one or two jars, cover them completely with olive oil, and leave to cool. Add a couple of chillies to each jar, if using. Then put on well-fitting lids and store in a cool, dark place.
TO SERVE You can use these as an hors d'œuvre or appetizer, with good bread to mop up the wonderful juices.

MENUS

The sequence and balance of a meal is as important as the taste of the food itself, and as much care should go into thinking about the character and impact of the dishes in relation to each other as the culinary skill required to prepare them. It is not only the stomachs but also the emotions of your guests you have to think of.

The first course should titillate and excite, the main course satisfy and intrigue, and the pudding induce, at its best, sheer ecstasy. Although you may want to concentrate on one national cuisine or theme – you may want to produce an Indian buffet for a party or a typically Italian family supper, for example – the individual dishes should contrast with and complement each other, not just in their taste, but by considering texture, colour, shape and even temperature. It may seem obvious, for instance, that you would not choose to sit down and eat three creamy, pale-coloured dishes one after another, but it is surprising how often just this sort of menu is offered simply through lack of forethought.

It can be particularly difficult to get a mix of tastes and textures in a completely vegetarian dinner party or family lunch menu. A mixture of different but complementary vegetable dishes can be successful,

but a focal centrepiece of some kind always gives more shape to the occasion. If you choose something like a vegetable pie, the accompanying vegetables should not clash with it. You wouldn't want to serve a carrot and sweetcorn pie, accompanied by more root or podded vegetables, for example. Leafy greens would be far more suitable. Even more than with a meal containing meat or fish, vegetable dishes must be of different character and colour.

When you are putting together a menu, it is also important to judge people's appetites. The first course must never be enough actually to satisfy hunger; in fact, it should remind people of the pleasure of eating and make them look forward even more to the rest of the meal. The main course should, by contrast, never leave you still feeling hungry, but you should not feel bloated either. If you are just about full, room can somehow always be found for a tempting pudding – and if you have served a rich main course, the pudding should be light and refreshing. If the main course is light, you may wish to serve a extra course – a salad, perhaps, or cheese before the pudding.

On the following pages there are some suggestions for menus – vegetarian and non-vegetarian (or 'almost vegetarian') – for a variety of occasions.

BRUNCH

*Brunch is rather a nice idea for holidays when you want to get up late and have
one meal which combines two. It is a far more formal meal than breakfast and
guests are usually invited, but it can also be very relaxed.*

FOR NON-VEGETARIANS

Three-cheese custard *(38)*

Smoked fish and sesame balls with tomato sauce *(84)*

Baked sandwiched aubergines *(53)*

White pear cake *(139)*

FOR VEGETARIANS

Egg, cheese and onion gratin with cherry tomatoes *(43)*

Dried broad bean purée with green vegetables *(55)*

Braised red cabbage with chestnuts and petits pois *(50)*

Carrot tart with candied carrot topping *(139)*

CHILDREN'S LUNCH

*With fussy children, meals can be tricky. However, they always seem to like
cheesy dishes, pasta and chicken. Even children who are difficult about eating
vegetables seem to accept them when they are combined with these things.*

FOR NON-VEGETARIANS

Vietnamese chicken noodle hotpot
with fresh leaves *(95)*

Ken Buggy's soda bread *(145)*

Soft berry fruits in passion fruit
fromage frais *(131)*

FOR VEGETARIANS

Leek and red onion cobbler
with potato and cheese pastry *(121)*
OR
Spaghetti with peas, spring onions and pea, mint and
smetana sauce *(32)*

Honey-glazed fresh apricot tart *(135)*

PICNIC

*Picnic food must be portable. However, some dishes can be carried in the pan
or dish they were made in, and kept warm, which always seems a special treat on
a chilly day. Above all, you must avoid sandwiches!*

FOR NON-VEGETARIANS

Exotic chicken pie *(105)*

Anchovy, garlic and parsley sticks *(148)*

Greek salad bread *(147)*

Squidgy prune, pecan, citrus
and honey cake *(143)*

FOR VEGETARIANS

Lentil tart with rice crunch pastry *(34)*

Devonian Spanish omelette *(43)*

Tomato, herb, Parmesan and garlic bread with
olive oil *(151)*

Citrus-drenched cake *(143)*

SUNDAY LUNCH

A Sunday morning spent listening to music and cooking for my family and friends is one of my favourite times. Sunday lunch is an informal, relaxed affair; it needs no first course, but to me a proper pudding is essential.

FOR NON-VEGETARIANS

Roast chicken with courgette and cranberry sauce *(105)*

Tuscan broad beans *(53)*

Goddess of Puddings *(141)*

FOR VEGETARIANS

Garden pie *(121)*

Sautéed leeks with pumpkin seeds and steamed sugar snap peas *(57)*

Sharp lemon soufflé on a chocolate shortbread base *(137)*

SUMMER LUNCH

When weather and location permit, it is pleasant to eat in the garden. Even if you can't, the food should make the most of seasonal ingredients. You can have several smaller dishes for a vegetarian meal instead of a heavier main course.

FOR NON-VEGETARIANS

New potatoes with quails' eggs and herby cream cheese mayonnaise *(15)*

Stuffed salmon with Mediterranean sauce *(75)*

Peach, rocket and mixed leaf salad with rose petals and rose water dressing *(59)*

Honey-glazed fresh apricot tart *(135)*

FOR VEGETARIANS

Chilled courgette, avocado and yogurt soup *(21)*

Fresh plum tomato and basil tart with olive oil and garlic crust *(9)*

Anglo-Syrian bread *(147)*

Green salad with spring flowers *(65)*

Rose petal sorbet with crystallized petals *(141)*

FAMILY SUPPER

Cosy and informal, this is almost my favourite kind of meal. It is a chance to make delicious dishes which need eating immediately and are impractical for formal meals or larger gatherings - and you can forget about a first course, too.

FOR NON-VEGETARIANS

Chicken and spinach pasta pie *(31)*

Chicory, avocado, cherry tomato and walnut salad *(68)*

Upside-down apple tart with orange and oatmeal pastry *(126)*

FOR VEGETARIANS

Cauliflower cheese with sun-dried tomatoes, fresh red chili and crunchy Parmesan topping *(37)*

Sautéed leeks with pumpkin seeds and steamed sugar snap peas *(57)*

White pear cake *(139)*

FORMAL DINNER PARTY

A formal dinner party can be very enjoyable to prepare. But in order to feel relaxed, shop the day before, and make the first course or the pudding well in advance too. The dishes should have a minimum of last-minute cooking.

FOR NON-VEGETARIANS

Pink trout balls with dill vinaigrette *(16)*

Pumpkin stuffed with spiced turkey and cashew nuts *(93)*

Chinese salad with bean sprouts and crispy spiced garlic *(67)*

Fromage frais and dark chocolate ice cream cake *(125)*

FOR VEGETARIANS

Avocados in spinach jelly with garlic and chilli *(15)*

Leek and aubergine charlotte with sun-dried tomatoes *(109)*

Sautéed mushrooms and broccoli with garlic and coriander seeds *(49)*

Raspberry and orange parfait in a chocolate case *(129)*

SUMMER BUFFET PARTY

Buffet parties usually offer too many different dishes. Since people often put a little of everything on their plates, it is vital to plan dishes which enhance each other. Prepare the food in advance and either eat cold or reheated.

FOR NON-VEGETARIANS

Prawn and smoked haddock mousse with scallop sauce *(12)*

Chicory, avocado, cherry tomato and walnut salad *(68)*

Steamed chicken balls with coriander leaf mayonnaise *(99)*

Green salad with spring flowers *(65)*

Apricot, rosemary and honey soufflé *(126)*

A bowl of raspberries or strawberries and a bowl of crème fraîche

FOR VEGETARIANS

Exotic egg and cucumber salad with coconut and yogurt sauce *(67)*

Shallot and spring onion tart with crunchy hot butter pastry *(11)*

Wild rice salad with cucumber and fresh orange *(71)*

Chick pea, feta cheese and tomato salad with green chili and lemon dressing *(73)*

Chocolate cake with vanilla and cinnamon *(143)*

A bowl of raspberries or strawberries and a bowl of crème fraîche

INDEX

THE AUTHOR

Josceline Dimbleby is one of Britain's most popular and most innovative food writers. Her books have sold more than 2 million copies in the UK alone. She is food correspondent of the *Sunday Telegraph* and contributes regularly to other newspapers and magazines. She also appears on television in programmes such as 'Masterchef' and 'Food & Drink'. She is particularly noted for the inventiveness and originality of her recipes which often feature brilliantly successful and unexpected combinations of ingredients. Josceline spent much of her childhood abroad, especially in the Middle East and in South America and she has travelled extensively in India and the Far East. Her unceasing flow of new ideas for recipes comes in part from her familiarity with a wide range of international cuisines.

Editorial Director Sandy Carr
Recipes Editor Pam Cary
Assistant Editor Anne Cochrane
Art Director Jason Vrakas
Art Editor Sara Kidd
Design Assistant Adelle Morris
Photographer Simon Wheeler
Home Economist Allyson Birch
Assistants to Allyson Birch Teresa Goldfinch,
Jane Stevenson
Stylist Rebecca Gillies
Indexer Naomi Good
Production Charles James

The author and publishers would like to thank the following people who helped
to test the recipes:

Anne Bailey, Matthew Barrell, Lorna Bateson, Andrew Christodolo,
Penny and Luke Cunliffe, Gemma Hancock, Sara Harper, Fiona Holman,
Paul Jackson, Charles and Saskia James, Rosanna Merrell, Suzanne Morris,
Lyn Parry, Margaret Rand, Clifford Rosen, John Worsfold